GREENFEAST

AUTUMN, WINTER

Also by Nigel Slater:

Greenfeast: Spring, summer
The Christmas Chronicles
The Kitchen Diaries III: A Year of Good Eating
Eat
The Kitchen Diaries II
Tender, Volumes I and II
Eating for England
The Kitchen Diaries I
Toast: The Story of a Boy's Hunger
Appetite
Real Food
Real Cooking
The 30-Minute Cook
Real Fast Food

Nigel Slater is an award-winning author, journalist, and television presenter. He has been food columnist for the *Observer* for over twenty-five years. His collection of bestselling books includes the classics *Appetite* and *The Kitchen Diaries* and the critically acclaimed two-volume *Tender*. He has made cooking shows and documentaries for BBC1, BBC2, and BBC4. His memoir *Toast: The Story of a Boy's Hunger* won six major awards and is now a film and stage production. His writing has won the James Beard Award, the National Book Award, the Glenfiddich Trophy, the André Simon Memorial Prize, and the British Biography of the Year. He lives in London.

nigelslater.com
Twitter @nigelslater
Instagram @nigelslater

GREENFEAST

AUTUMN, WINTER

Nigel Slater

Photographs by
Jonathan Lovekin

TEN SPEED PRESS
California | New York

Ten Speed Press and the Ten Speed Press colophon are registered trademarks of
Penguin Random House LLC.

Originally published in the United Kingdom in 2019

Library of Congress Cataloging-in-Publication Data is on file with the publisher.

Hardcover ISBN: 978-1-984-858-733
eBook ISBN: 978-1-984-858-740

Printed in China

Interior design by David Pearson
Cover design by Lizzie Allen

10 9 8 7 6 5 4 3 2

First U.S. Edition

For James

TOM KEMP

Tom Kemp has had a couple of careers. He trained formally as a theoretical computer scientist and followed a sequence of postdoctoral research and programming posts. In parallel, he was learning to be an artist by studying the writings of ancient manuscripts, not their content but how they were made. In particular, he worked out the details of a Roman signwriting technique that has informed all his brushwork, both readable and abstract. This calligraphic training led to a deeper pursuit of writing in general and artworks in many media, including graffiti and digital work. Along the way he learned to make porcelain vessels on a potter's wheel, an activity he describes as "calligraphy in 3D," and these now form the large surfaces on which he continues to write.

tomkemp.com
Instagram @tom_kemp_

CONTENTS

Introduction xiv

Winter Basics 1
In a Pan 9
On Toast 45
In the Oven 65
On a Plate 131
With a Crust 143
With a Ladle 163
On the Stove 193
Dessert 241

Index 286
Acknowledgments 296
A note on the Brushstrokes 300
A note on the Type 302

INTRODUCTION

Dinner is different in winter. The change starts late on a summer's evening, when you first notice the soft, familiar scent of distant woodsmoke in the sudden chill of the evening air. Then, a day or two later, a damp, mushroomy mist hovers over the gardens and parks. Later, you notice the leaves have turned silently from yellow ocher to walnut. Autumn is here once again. You may sigh, rejoice, or open a bottle. For many, this is the end of their year. For me, this is when it starts, when warmth and bonhomie come to the fore. Energy returns.

With the change of weather, supper takes on a more significant role. We are suddenly hungry. Once the nights draw in, I am no longer satisfied by plates of milky burrata and slices of sweet, apricot-fleshed melon. No more am I content with a bowl of couscous with peaches, soft cheese, and herbs for dinner. What I crave now is food that is both comforting and warming, substantial and deeply satisfying. Food that nourishes but also sets me up for going back out in the cold and wet. And yet, I still find my diet is heavily plant-based with less emphasis on meat. It is simply the way it has progressed over the years, and it shows little sign of abating.

At the start of the longest half of the year, our appetite is pricked by the sudden drop in temperature, and as evenings get longer, we have the opportunity to spend a little more time in the kitchen. To mash beans into buttery clouds. To simmer vegetable stews to serve with bowls of couscous. To bring dishes of sweet potato to melting tenderness in spiced cream. And of course, the pasta jar comes out again.

My cold-weather eating is more substantial than the food I eat for the rest of the year. Dinner becomes about one main dish rather than several lighter ones, and the focus shifts toward keeping warm. On returning home I will now happily spend an hour cooking. Maybe a little longer.

The oven gets more use at this time of year, the grill and griddle probably less. More food will come to the table in deep casseroles and pie dishes. I dig out my capacious ladle for a creamed celery root soup as soft as velvet. The temperature of the plates and bowls will change. We want to hold things that warm our hands, a sign of the happiness to come.

There will be carbs. They protect and energize us. They bring balm to our jagged nerves. (Winter is nature's way of making us eat carbohydrates.) Crusts — of pastry, breadcrumbs, and crumble — add substance, potatoes fill and satisfy, and there is once again a huge sourdough loaf on the table. Rice and noodles are no longer a side dish and now become the heart and soul of dinner.

My autumn and winter cooking is every bit as plant-based as the food I make in the summer; it just has a bit more heft to it. Shallow bowls of rice cooked with milk and thyme in the style of a risotto. A verdant, filling soup of Brussels sprouts and blue cheese. A saffron-colored stew of sour cream, herbs, and noodles. Translucent fritters in a pool of melted cheese. Golden mushrooms astride a cloud of soft yellow polenta. There is a tangle of noodles and tomato, peppery with chile; roast parsnips and baked pumpkin; a wide earthenware dish of sweet potatoes and lentils glowing like a lantern; an herb-freckled crumble of leeks and tomato or rutabagas and thyme in a pastry crust; and a tarte Tatin of soft golden shallots and autumn apples. It is all here, between these covers.

This is also the season for "something on toast." By toast I mean not only bread cut thick and rough-edged, but toasted bagels and crumpets, muffins and naan. Any soft dough that will crisp under the broiler and will support a cargo of vegetables or is happy to be slathered with a thick wave of crème fraîche or hummus, roast vegetables, or perhaps cheese to melt and bubble.

And, of course, there must be dessert. An early-autumn crumble of plums and almonds. Chocolate puddings (you really must make the ones with dulce de leche). Ginger cake with a cardamom cream, and a custard set with cake and apples. There will be nut-encrusted shortbreads with blood orange, and baked apples with crisp crumbs and cranberries. I expect syllabubs and baked pears on the table, pastries laden with a golden dice of apples, and scones pebble-dashed with nibs of dark chocolate.

I probably eat more desserts during the cold months, but mainly on the weekend. The main-course recipes in this book are predominantly for two; the desserts, though, are all for four or more. You can't really make a tart for two or a tiny batch of scones. The recipes are made for sharing with friends and family. That said, most of them are rather fine eaten the following day. Especially those little chocolate puddings.

Like all my books, the first volume of *Greenfeast* was written from and about my own kitchen. That it found itself welcomed by quite so many came as something of a pleasant surprise. I have lost count of the number of people who in the last few months have told me that this is the way they eat now, as an "almost vegetarian."

The idea that so many people's everyday eating is going through such a change, and that meat is no longer our first thought when working out what we want to eat, is heartening to say the least. Apparently I am not the only person for whom meat is still looked forward to but as a once- or twice-a-week treat, not the knee-jerk star of every meal. I knew this was happening (you would have to live under a stone not to) but I genuinely hadn't realized how widely and quickly the change has come about.

Yes, vegan cooking and full-blown vegetarianism is on the rise, but there are far more people who seem to prefer a less rigid approach to their eating. This makes sense on so many levels, but when all is said and eaten, it is simply that the options for cooking without meat have never been more varied or delicious. There has never been a better time to celebrate the move toward a mostly plant-based diet.

WINTER BASICS

WINTER STOCK

A good vegetable stock is worth its weight in gold on a winter's day. As the nights draw in, we probably need a stock altogether deeper, richer, and more ballsy than the delicate vegetal liquids we might use in summer. Something that behaves more like a brown meat stock. Such a broth is immensely useful in my kitchen as a base for the heartier non-meat recipes that form the backbone of my daily eating, but also as something restoring to drink as you might a cup of miso. The color must be dark and glossy, the flavor deeply, mysteriously herbal with a hint of mushroom, and there should be a roasted back note, the sort you find in a long-simmered meat stock.

As you proceed, the kitchen will fill with the smell of onions, celery, and carrots, which you roast with miso paste, then remove from the oven and simmer for a good hour with thyme, bay, and shiitake. You could slip in a sheet of kombu for an extra layer of depth if you like.

The broth will need straining and separating from its spent aromatics, its deep, almost mahogany liquor dripping slowly into a glass bowl. The liquor can be used immediately or kept in the fridge, covered, for up to a week.

Such a stock is a bowl of pure treasure. You can drink it like broth, dipping thick hunks of bread or focaccia into it. You can use it as a base for a soup, adding steamed cauliflower or shredded cabbage, parsley, and croutons, or add noodles, skeins of udon, or little pasta stars to twinkle in the dark, mushroomy depths. Whenever the word *stock* appears in a recipe, use it neat or dilute it with a little water to taste. And it will freeze too, though I suggest in small containers, so it defrosts quickly.

And when all is said and done, is there anything quite so restoring as coming home to a bowl of deeply layered, smoky stock to bubble on the stove, to which you add pieces of hot toast, letting them slowly swell with the bosky, fungal, roasted flavors from the bowl?

WINTER PORRIDGE

A winter's day should start well. A steaming bowl of something to see us on our way. I invariably choose porridge. An oat-based slop to satisfy and strengthen, to bolster and soothe, to see me through till I get where I'm going. A sort of internal down coat. I doubt it will just be porridge of course, but porridge with bells and whistles: a trickle of treacle, a pool of crème fraîche, ribbons of maple syrup, or a puddle of yogurt. There may be golden raisins and dried mulberries, pistachios, or toasted almonds and perhaps some baked figs or slices of banana.

Porridge doesn't necessarily mean oats. You could use rye grain or barley and milk or water as you wish. There might be salt or sugar, cinnamon or ground cardamom, or toasted pumpkin seeds. There will be stewed fruit too: apples perhaps, or dried apricots cooked with sugar or honey. Porridge is never just porridge in my house. It is a winter staple, one of the building blocks of the season and something I could never think of being without.

A BROWN VEGETABLE STOCK

Deep flavors. An herbal, umami-rich stock for winter cooking.

Makes about 2 quarts/2 liters

onions, medium 2
carrots 9 oz/250g
celery 2 sticks
garlic a small, whole head
light miso paste 3 tablespoons
water ⅓ cup/80ml, plus
   3 quarts/3 liters

dried shiitake mushrooms
   1¾ oz/50g
rosemary 5 sprigs
thyme 10 sprigs
bay leaves 3
black peppercorns 12
dried kombu ⅓ oz/10g

Set the oven at 400°F/180°C. Peel and roughly chop the onions, then place in a roasting pan together with the skins. Similarly chop the carrots and celery sticks, then mix with the onions and the head of garlic, separated into cloves.

Mix together the miso paste and ⅓ cup/80ml of water, then stir into the vegetables, coating them lightly. Bake for about 1 hour, tossing the vegetables once or twice during cooking, until everything is brown, fragrant, and toasty.

Transfer the roasted vegetables and aromatics to a deep saucepan. Add the shiitake, rosemary, thyme, bay, peppercorns, and kombu, then pour a little of the 3 quarts/3 liters of water into the roasting pan, scrape at the caramelized bits stuck to the pan, then pour into the saucepan. Add the remaining water. Bring to a boil, then lower the heat and simmer, partially covered with a lid, for fifty minutes to 1 hour.

When you have a deep brown, richly colored broth, tip through a sieve into a heatproof bowl or large pitcher and let cool. Refrigerate and use as necessary.

• Keeps for up to one week in the fridge.

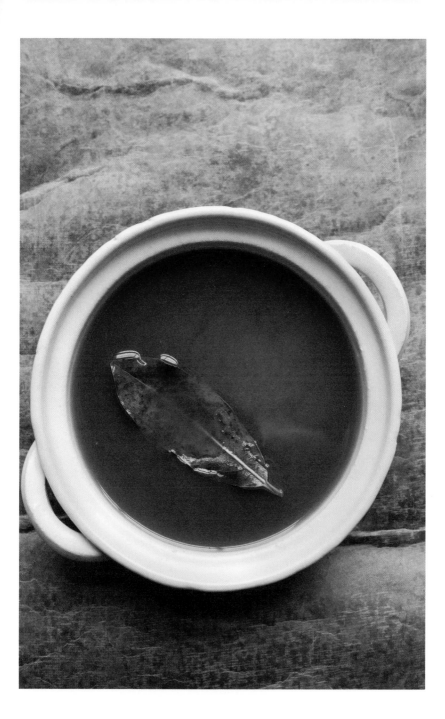

OATS, DRIED MULBERRIES, DATE SYRUP

The solace of porridge. The sweetness of dried fruits.

Serves 2

rolled oats 1 cup/100g
water 1⅔ cups/400ml
dried mulberries ⅓ cup/50g
golden raisins ½ cup/75g

heavy cream or crème fraîche
  ¼ cup/60ml
date syrup 2 tablespoons

Put the oats and water into a small saucepan and bring to a boil. Add a good pinch of salt and stir the oats continuously for four or five minutes with a wooden spoon until the porridge is thick and creamy.

Divide between two bowls, then add the dried mulberries and golden raisins. Add spoonfuls of cream or crème fraîche, then trickle with the date syrup.

• I often use dried apricots in place of the mulberries, but cranberries and dried cherries are good alternatives.
• The sweetness of the date syrup can be balanced by a spoon or two of stewed tart apples.

IN A PAN

On a winter's evening, I warm butter and olive oil in a shallow-sided cast-iron pan, turn the heat down low, and use it to fry thin slices of potato, Jerusalem artichoke, or fennel. Vegetables that will crisp or soften as you wish, and to which I can add other ingredients at will — sweet black grapes and whole parsley leaves to the crisp artichokes; peas and salty cheese to the softened fennel. I do the same with slices of pumpkin or butternut squash, then introduce feta or breadcrumbs or perhaps a fried egg whose yolk will double as an impromptu sauce.

A heavy frying pan in which you can leave things to cook at a moderate temperature is worth its weight in gold. It is the gift I would give to a kid leaving home. The possibilities are endless. Mushrooms, sliced and sautéed with herbs to pile on a mound of silken hummus; beans whose outsides slowly crisp in olive oil and are then tossed with tomatoes and a wobbly egg of burrata; Brussels sprouts fried with miso paste to a deep walnut brown, then forked through sticky brown rice. They all give a substantial green and deeply savory supper.

The success often lies in the pan itself. A pitted or wobbly-bottomed pan will produce uneven results. Sometimes you need a thin-bottomed pan in which to flash-fry, other times a pan as heavy as possible that will hold the heat and which can be left to do its task while you get on with other elements of dinner. Choose your weapon.

It is worth finding a suitable lid. Especially if you are cooking vegetables that need to be brought gently to tenderness before a final crisping, such as potatoes, parsnips, and carrots. The sort of heavyweight pans I find so useful for slow winter cooking often come without a lid, so it is not a bad idea to find one that fits before you leave the shop.

I am very fond of my old cast-iron sauté pans, but they do need a bit of care when you first get them home. A good oiling with vegetable oil, a long, slow bake in the oven, and a careful dry before putting them away will give them a chance to develop a patina, a naturally nonstick layer that will, unlike a commercial nonstick finish, see you through a lifetime of suppers.

ARTICHOKES, BEANS, GREEN OLIVES

Crisp beans and fried artichokes. Dinner from the deli.

Serves 2

green olives, pitted
   1½ cups/200g
olive oil 7 tablespoons/100ml
basil 20 leaves
lemon juice 5 tablespoons/75ml
parsley leaves from a small bunch
black garlic 2 cloves

olive oil, for frying 2 tablespoons
navy beans 1 × 15-oz/400g can
fine ground polenta
   6 tablespoons/50g
eggs 2
artichokes in oil 12¼ oz/350g
peanut oil, for deep frying

Put the olives into the jug of a blender, then add the olive oil, basil leaves, lemon juice, parsley leaves, and black garlic. Blend to a thick purée.

Warm the olive oil for frying in a shallow pan that doesn't stick, drain the beans, and add them to the pan, then let them cook over moderate heat, turning occasionally, until they are lightly crisp.

Put the polenta on a large plate. Break the eggs into a shallow dish and mix the yolks and whites together lightly with a fork. If the artichokes are whole, then slice them in half. Roll each half in the beaten egg, then place in the polenta and turn over, pressing down firmly to coat evenly.

Heat the peanut oil, add the artichokes, and fry till golden and crisp. Lift each from the oil and drain briefly on paper towels before dividing between two plates. Serve with the crisp beans and the olive paste and, if you wish, a wedge of lemon.

• Make a black olive paste if you prefer, using pitted black olives. I would also be tempted to add a pinch of dried chile flakes when you blend the ingredients.
• You can use breadcrumbs instead of polenta. Sieve fresh dry crumbs onto a plate and roll the artichokes in them after coating in egg.

EGGPLANTS, GINGER, TAMARIND

Hot, sweet, sour.

Serves 2

lime juice 7 tablespoons/100ml
   (from about 2 limes)
ginger 1 oz/30g
fish sauce 1 tablespoon
palm sugar 4 teaspoons
hot red chile 1
hot green chile 1
tamarind paste 4 teaspoons
peanut oil 2 tablespoons

eggplants 10½ oz/300g

For the apple yogurt:
mint leaves 12
a small apple
white wine vinegar 2 tablespoons
plain whole milk yogurt
   ¾ cup/190g

Put the lime juice into a large bowl. Peel and grate the ginger, stirring the resulting paste into the lime juice. Pour in the fish sauce, then stir in the palm sugar until dissolved.

Finely chop the red and green chiles, removing the seeds if you wish, then add them to the marinade with the tamarind paste and peanut oil, combining the ingredients thoroughly.

Cut the eggplants in half lengthwise, then into wedges, as you might a melon. Now cut each wedge in half. Put the eggplants into the marinade, turn to coat, and set aside for a good half hour. During this time they will soften a little.

Make the apple yogurt: finely chop the mint leaves and put them in a small mixing bowl. Grate the apple into the bowl (it can be as coarse or as fine as you wish), then stir in the white wine vinegar and yogurt, cover, and set aside.

To cook the eggplants, heat a cast-iron griddle (and switch on the extractor vent above the stove). Place the eggplants on the griddle and let

(continued)

brown on the underside. Turn, loosening them from the griddle with an offset spatula, and brown the other side. Keep the heat low to moderate, and make sure they are cooked right through — they must be fully tender.

Serve the eggplants, hot from the griddle, with the apple yogurt sauce.

• Cut the eggplants in slices or wedges, as the fancy takes you. There will, I assure you, be much smoke, so switch on the extractor or open a window. Better still, cook the eggplants outside on the barbecue. Arm yourself with an offset spatula to gently pry them from the bars of the griddle. I like to keep the heat no hotter than medium to give the eggplant time to cook through to the middle, a process you can speed up by covering the eggplant with an upturned metal bowl (or a lid, if your griddle has one). If you prefer, rather than the sour apple dressing, make a dressing of olive oil, lime juice, and cilantro leaves.

• A twist of noodles, tossed with the merest splash of sesame oil, could be a suitable accompaniment here, as would long-grain rice, steamed and seasoned with black pepper and sesame seeds.

BRUSSELS SPROUTS, BROWN RICE, MISO

The savor of miso. The homeliness of brown rice.

Serves 2–3

brown sushi rice 1 cup/190g
Brussels sprouts 1 lb 10 oz/750g
peanut oil 2 tablespoons

light miso paste 1 tablespoon
Japanese pickles (tsukemono)
  2 tablespoons

Put the rice in a bowl, cover with warm water, then run your fingers through the grains. Drain, repeat, then tip into a saucepan, cover with 2 inches/5cm of cold water, and set aside for half an hour.

Wash and trim the sprouts, then cut each in half. Bring the soaked rice to a boil in its soaking water, add half a teaspoon of salt, cover, and lower the heat so the water simmers. Cook for thirty minutes or until the rice is approaching tenderness. Remove the pan from the heat and let rest for ten minutes before removing the lid.

Warm the oil in a shallow pan. Toss the sprouts with the miso paste, then transfer to the hot oil, moving them round the pan as they become crisp and pale golden brown.

Remove the lid from the rice, run a fork through the grains to separate them, then divide between two or three bowls. Spoon the miso sprouts into the rice and add some of the Japanese pickles.

• Fried in a little oil, the miso paste forms a fine crust on the outside of the sprouts. Serve them as an accompaniment if you wish, but I like them as the star of the show, tucked into a bowl of sticky rice and scattered with salty Japanese pickles. I serve this as it is, but also as a side dish for slices of cold roast pork and its crackling. This is sticky rice, my favorite, but you don't want it in lumps, so running the tines of a fork through the cooked grain is a good idea.

BURRATA, BEANS, TOMATOES

Milky snow-white cheese. Toasted beans. Peppery basil.

Serves 2

garlic 3 cloves
olive oil
cannellini beans 1 × 15-oz/
    400g can

cherry tomatoes 9 oz/250g
basil leaves a handful
burrata 2 × 9-oz/250g balls

Flatten the garlic cloves with the blade of a kitchen knife, then peel away the skins. Warm ¼ cup/60ml of olive oil in a shallow pan and add the garlic, letting it cook briefly over moderate heat. Drain the cannellini beans.

Cut the tomatoes in half, pour a little more oil into the pan, then add the tomatoes and the drained cannellini. Fry briefly, for four or five minutes, until the beans are starting to crisp a little.

Tear the basil leaves and add to the beans, stirring them in gently, until they start to wilt. Divide the beans and tomatoes between two plates, add the burrata, and trickle with olive oil.

• The beans will crisp deliciously around the edges if you allow them to fry in the hot oil. Stirring them too often will cause them to break up as they develop their golden shell.
• Cannellini beans are my first choice here, but lima beans are worth considering too. Green flageolet don't seem to work quite as well, though I am not entirely sure why.
• This is one of the lighter recipes in this volume, yet each time I make it, I am surprised by how satisfying it is.

BUTTERNUT, BREADCRUMBS, CURRY POWDER

Sweet golden squash. Warm, spicy curry. Crisp crumbs.

Serves 2

onions, medium 2
carrots, large 10½ oz/300g
peanut oil 3 tablespoons
butternut squash 1 lb 2 oz/500g
curry powder 2 teaspoons
ground turmeric 1 teaspoon

vegetable stock 2 cups plus
  2 tablespoons/500ml
panko breadcrumbs
  6 tablespoons
parsley, chopped ¼ cup/5g
togarashi 1–2 teaspoons

Peel and roughly chop the onions and carrots, then put them in a large saucepan with the oil and place over moderate heat. Let the vegetables cook for ten to fifteen minutes, until the onions are pale gold.

Slice the butternut into ¾-inch/2cm-thick rounds, remove the seeds, and peel it if you wish. When the onions are nicely golden, stir in the curry powder, ground turmeric, and a little salt and fry briefly, then pour in the vegetable stock and bring to a boil. Tuck in the slices of squash and lower the heat to a simmer. Cook for fifteen minutes, then remove the squash and place half of the sauce in a blender. Process to a smooth purée, then return to the pan and keep at a low bubble for five minutes.

Toast the panko crumbs in a dry pan till golden, then toss with the chopped parsley and togarashi. Slide the squash back into the sauce for a couple of minutes, sprinkle with the parsley crumbs, then serve.

• Togarashi, the Japanese spice mix, can be found in major supermarkets, Japanese food shops, and online.
• The sauce is based on a classic katsu, which flatters the sweetness of the butternut. You can turn up the heat if you wish with a little more togarashi seasoning or even a splash of chile sauce.
• Also try the sauce with baked eggplant or roasted parsnips.

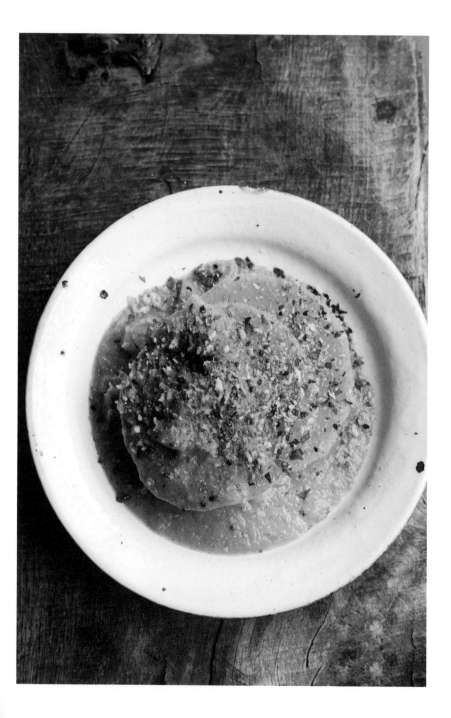

BUTTERNUT, FETA, EGGS

Crisp, light, sweet, salty.

Makes 9 fritters. Serves 3

butternut squash 10½ oz/300g
garlic 2 cloves
peanut oil
eggs 2
feta cheese 7 oz/200g
all-purpose flour ¼ cup/30g

thyme leaves, chopped
    1 tablespoon
parsley, chopped 3 heaped
    tablespoons
peanut or vegetable oil,
    for deep frying

Peel and remove the seeds from the butternut squash. Push the squash through a spiralizer to create long, thin strings.

Peel the garlic and thinly slice it. Warm a little peanut oil in a large, shallow pan, then add the garlic, let it sizzle for a couple of minutes, and then, as it starts to color, drop in the squash and fry for five or six minutes till the colors are bright and the squash is tender but far from falling apart.

Separate the eggs. Make a batter by mixing together the egg yolks, crumbled feta cheese, flour, a grinding of black pepper, and the chopped thyme leaves and parsley. Beat the egg whites till frothy, then fold into the batter. Toss the threads of butternut with the batter.

Warm enough peanut oil in a deep, heavy pan to fry the fritters. When the oil is at 355°F/180°C, take a large spoonful of the batter-coated butternut and lower into the hot oil. Repeat with another three or four, frying for three or four minutes till crisp and golden in color. As each fritter is ready, remove with a draining spoon and rest on paper towels. Continue with spoonfuls of the batter until you have nine fritters. Serve hot.

• So good are these little fritters that I have tried them with other vegetables too, including shredded zucchini (a success) and beet (less so). It is worth having something to dip them into, such as a cucumber, mint, and yogurt dip or a bowl of especially creamy hummus.

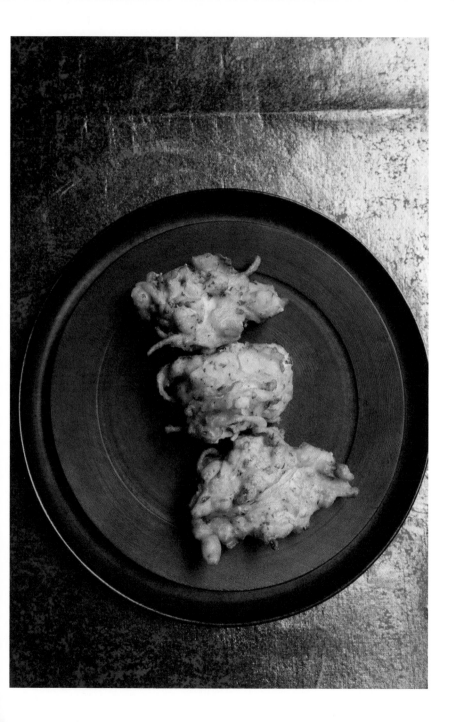

EGGS, EDAMAME, BEAN SPROUTS

A soft pillow of egg. A tangle of vegetables.

Serves 2

edamame beans, shelled
 7 oz/200g
green onions 8
bok choy 7 oz/200g
garlic 3 cloves
large green chiles 2

peanut oil ¼ cup/60ml
bean sprouts 7 oz/200g
eggs 6
nigella seeds 2 teaspoons
cilantro a handful

Bring a pan of water to a boil, add the edamame, and boil till tender —
about eight minutes. Drain and refresh in a bowl of ice water.

Finely chop the green onions, discarding the roots and any tough dark
green leaves. Shred the bok choy. Peel and thinly slice the garlic. Finely
slice the chiles.

Warm half the peanut oil in a large, shallow pan, fry the green onions,
garlic, and chiles till soft, then add the shredded bok choy and lastly the
bean sprouts, tossing them in the hot oil and cooking for three or four
minutes till softened.

Break the eggs into a bowl and beat them lightly with a fork. Add the
cooked and drained edamame and the fried vegetables. Season with a
little sea salt and black pepper and fold in the nigella seeds and cilantro.

Warm the remaining oil in a large ovensafe frying pan, pour in the
omelette mixture, and fry over moderate heat for about eight minutes,
until the edges have set and the middle is still almost liquid. Heat the
oven broiler. Place the frying pan under the broiler and continue cooking
for two or three minutes until the center of the omelette is lightly set.
(Ideally, it should be a little runny, verging on the point of setting.) Cut
in half and serve. *(continued)*

• To the basic mixture you can add pretty much any vegetable you have on hand, from fried mushrooms to steamed shredded cabbage. The cooking time is brief, so most vegetables will have to be lightly cooked first. Brassicas such as long-stemmed sprouting broccoli work very well, as do any late autumn beans. I especially like steamed mustard greens.

FENNEL, PEAS, HALLOUMI

Fresh green flavors for a golden autumn day.

Serves 2
fennel 10½ oz/300g
olive oil 3 tablespoons
halloumi 9 oz/250g

For the dressing:
frozen peas 1⅔ cups/250g
basil leaves 1½ cups/30g
mint leaves 1 cup/20g
olive oil ¾ cup plus
    2 tablespoons/150ml

Trim and thinly slice the fennel, no thicker than one-eighth inch. Warm the three tablespoons of oil in your largest frying pan, place the fennel in the pan in a single layer, then season lightly with salt and cook until the fennel is light gold on the underside. Turn each piece over and continue cooking until soft and translucent.

Slice the halloumi into pieces slightly thicker than the fennel and place them in the pan, tucking them in wherever there is a gap, overlapping where there isn't. Let the cheese toast and turn patchily gold.

Put the frozen peas in a colander and run them under the cold tap for a few minutes till they have defrosted. Let them drain. Whiz the peas, basil and mint leaves, and the oil in a food processor till almost smooth — a slightly rough texture is good — then spoon over the cheese and fennel and serve. If you have a few fennel fronds, add them at the very end.

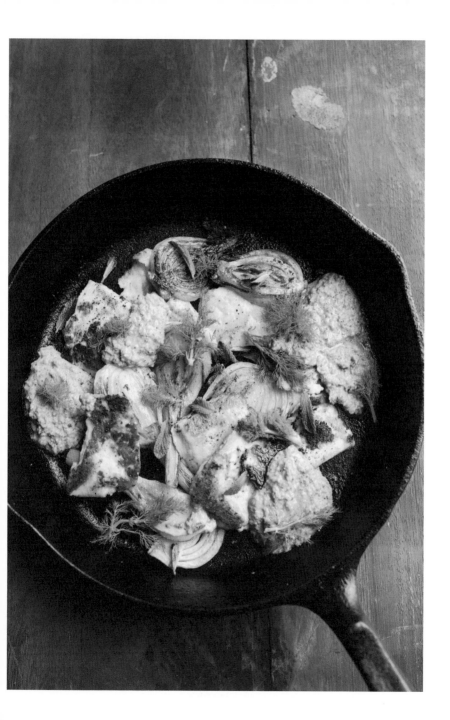

JERUSALEM ARTICHOKES, PISTACHIOS, GRAPES

Golden carbs. Black grapes.

Serves 2–3

a lemon
Jerusalem artichokes 7 oz/200g
shallots, small 6
black grapes 5¼ oz/150g

olive oil 3 tablespoons
golden raisins ¼ cup/35g
shelled pistachios ¼ cup/35g
parsley leaves a handful

Halve the lemon and squeeze the juice into a bowl. Peel the Jerusalem artichokes, then cut into rounds approximately ¼ inch thick. Put the artichokes into the bowl with the lemon juice and toss together. This will prevent the artichokes from going brown.

Peel the shallots and cut them in half from stem to root. Halve and seed the grapes. Warm the olive oil in your largest shallow pan. Add the artichokes and shallots to the hot oil, turning them over when their underside is golden and they are starting to soften.

As the artichokes become tender, add the grapes and raisins and lastly, the pistachios and parsley.

• Small potatoes can successfully replace the artichokes. You could also use parsnips. I find it best to use parsnips that have been steamed for ten minutes before frying. They are more tender that way.
• Should you find it easier, you can roast the artichokes instead of frying them, adding the remaining ingredients to the pan once the artichokes are golden.

MUSHROOMS, HUMMUS, HERBS

Creamed chickpeas. Sizzling mushrooms.

Serves 2

heavy cream 1 cup/240ml
chickpeas 1 × 15-oz/400g can
cilantro leaves and stems
   ½ cup/10g
dill ¾ cup/15g
parsley ½ cup/10g

king oyster mushrooms
   14 oz/400g
olive oil ¼ cup/60ml
butter 2 tablespoons
garlic 4 cloves

Warm the cream and drained chickpeas in a medium-sized saucepan for five minutes over moderate heat. Tip them into a blender or food processor with the cilantro, dill, and parsley and process to a thick cream. Transfer back to the saucepan and season with salt.

Slice the mushrooms into ½-inch/1cm-thick pieces. Warm the olive oil and butter in a shallow pan, add the slices of mushroom, and cook till golden on both sides. You may need to add a little more oil. As each mushroom browns, remove to a plate or piece of paper towel.

Peel and thinly slice the garlic, cook briefly in the pan until it turns gold, then return all the mushrooms to the pan. Warm the hummus, spoon onto plates, then add the sizzling mushrooms and garlic.

• Mushrooms, fried with butter and garlic, are just one possibility here; the soft, herb-speckled purée lends itself to sitting under deep-fried artichokes or roasted parsnips, baked tomatoes, or wedges of baked cabbage.
• Such purées can be made and kept in a small bowl overnight in the fridge, their surface splashed with olive oil and tightly covered. Stored like this, their texture will thicken and they can be spread on slices of hot toast for a quick bite to eat when you arrive home, hungry.

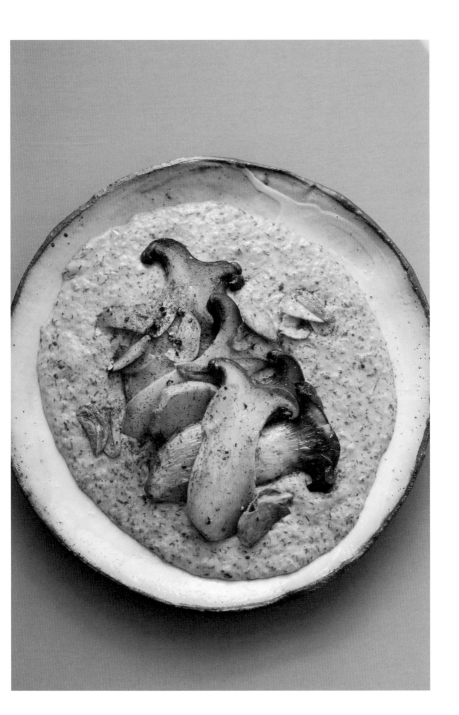

PARSLEY, PARMESAN, EGG

Warm, soft, parsley-freckled drop scones. (Pictured on page 39.)

Makes 6

parsley leaves ¾ cup/15g
all-purpose flour 1¼ cups plus
   3 tablespoons/180g
baking powder 2¾ teaspoons
salt ¼ teaspoon
a large egg

milk ¾ cup plus 3 tablespoons/
   220ml
parmesan, grated 5 heaped
   tablespoons/35g
butter a little

Roughly chop the parsley leaves. Put the flour in a large mixing bowl, add the baking powder and salt, and combine. (You can sift them together if you wish.) Break the egg into a bowl and beat lightly with a fork to combine white and yolk, mix in the milk, then stir into the flour.

Add the grated parmesan and chopped parsley to the batter. In a medium, nonstick or well-used frying pan, melt a couple tablespoons of butter over moderate heat. Pour in a sixth of the batter, making a round with a 2¾-inch/7cm diameter. Repeat with two more, then let them cook for two to four minutes, checking the underside regularly for color.

When they are puffed and golden, use an offset spatula to carefully turn each one over. Cook for another one to three minutes, then lift out and keep warm. A sound test for doneness is to touch the center of each scone with your finger. It should feel lightly springy. Continue with the remaining batter. Serve with the pumpkin hash on page 38.

• The drop scones can be flavored with chopped thyme or rosemary, basil, or tarragon. In which case I would serve them with grilled tomatoes, lightly crushed with a fork, or chopped spinach softened with a little cream.

PUMPKIN, ONIONS, ROSEMARY

Sweet and sticky squash.

Serves 6

pumpkin or butternut squash
1 lb 8 oz/700g
onions, medium 2

butter 2 tablespoons
olive oil 2 tablespoons
rosemary 3 sprigs

Peel the pumpkin and cut the flesh into cubes roughly 1¼ × 1¼ inches/ 3 × 3cm. Peel and roughly chop the onions. Warm the butter and olive oil in a large, shallow pan, add the pumpkin and onions and let them cook, with a regular stir, for about ten minutes. Finely chop the rosemary leaves, discarding the stalks, add to the pan with a little sea salt and coarsely ground black pepper, then cover with a lid and let cook over low to moderate heat for about fifteen minutes.

Check the onion and pumpkin occasionally to make sure they aren't browning too much. They are done when soft and easily crushed between your fingers. Serve with the drop scones on page 36.

• As well as a side dish for the drop scones, this can be used as the stuffing for an omelette or frittata, or served as a vegetable dish piled onto steamed rice.
• Use the recipe above with zucchini instead of pumpkin.

RAINBOW CHARD, EGG, NOODLES

A joyful tangle of noodles and greens.

Serves 2

a red chile, medium
a green chile, medium
a bunch of cilantro
    scant 1 oz/25g
garlic 1 clove
ginger a ½-oz/15g piece

rainbow chard 3½ oz/100g
eggs 3
peanut oil 5 tablespoons/75ml
cooked udon noodles
soy sauce to taste
sesame oil a dash

Thinly slice the chiles. Cut the cilantro stems into small pieces the length of a matchstick and reserve the leaves. Peel and thinly slice the garlic. Peel the ginger, then cut into skinny matchsticks. Remove the leaves from the chard and roughly shred them, then chop the stems into short pieces.

Break the eggs into a small bowl and beat them. Warm half the oil in a large, shallow pan over moderate heat, pour in the beaten egg and allow to set, checking the underside after a minute or two. When the omelette is golden, flip over and let the other side cook for a minute or two, then remove from the pan and tear the omelette into small pieces.

Wipe the pan clean with paper towels, add the remaining oil, and let it sizzle. Add the ginger, garlic, and chiles to the pan and fry till golden and fragrant. Add the cilantro and chard stems and continue cooking for two minutes, then add the soft noodles and toss everything together.

Stir in the soy sauce and a little sesame oil, add the chard and cilantro leaves and the torn omelette, and continue cooking for a minute till all is hot and sizzling.

TOFU, RADISH, PONZU

A gossamer-thin, crisp crust. Trembling tofu. A salty citrus dressing.

Serves 2

soft tofu 12 oz/340g
ponzu sauce ¼ cup/60ml
sesame oil 1 tablespoon
rice vinegar 3 tablespoons
green onion 1
radishes 4

cilantro leaves a handful
cornstarch or potato flour
⅓ cup/40g
ginger a thumb-sized lump
peanut or vegetable oil,
for deep frying

Drain the tofu on paper towels. Mix together the ponzu, sesame oil, and rice vinegar. Trim and finely chop the green onion, then thinly slice the radishes and add both to the dressing together with the cilantro leaves.

Put the cornstarch or potato flour into a shallow bowl or deep plate. Cut the tofu into six large cubes. Finely grate the ginger to a purée.

Warm the oil to 355°F/180°C in a deep pan. Gently toss the cubes of tofu in the cornstarch, then lower into the oil and fry for three or four minutes till light gold in color. Divide the dressing between two deep bowls, lift the tofu from the oil with a slotted spoon, then lower three pieces into each bowl. Top with the puréed ginger and eat while the tofu is still hot and crisp.

ON TOAST

Two little words. So much joy. I sometimes think *on toast* might be the best two words in the world. That slice of toast could be heavy with butter, shining pools forming on its surface; saturated with olive oil, glistening bright with crystals of sea salt; or perhaps its golden crust is shimmering with Marmite or honey.

Toast can be a round of "white sliced" popping up from the toaster; thick air-pocketed sourdough, its crust caught black under the broiler; neat rectangles of dark rye, all treacle and aniseed. Then again it could be a muffin, ripped rather than sliced in half, or a crumpet whose buttery cargo has trickled deep into its holes. Toast can be focaccia or ciabatta, fruit loaf or panettone, naan or roti. In short, any dough whose surface will toast crisply and hold something delicious.

I often tuck a piece of thick toast underneath a wedge of roasted pumpkin or eggplant, the bread soaking up the juices as the veg cooks. Almost anything, from broccoli you have cooked in butter on the stove to a stew whose juices deserve a thick pillow to soak them up, can be piled on top of toast.

It is difficult to think of anything more instantly satisfying than a thick wodge of golden bread under a pool of melted cheese. But that is just a start. I like to cook slices of leek or onion in butter till silky, then hide them underneath a layer of cheddar; mix grated beet and apple with goat cheese and sit it on sourdough or rye.

We can extend the very meaning of toast to include any piece of dough whose surface has been deliciously crisped by the heat. Many are the times I have commandeered everything from warm oatcakes to a white sliced loaf to use as a supporting role for cooked vegetables or melted cheese. Even a crumpet fits the bill, especially when spread with a layer of cream cheese and topped with lightly cooked spinach. And I could never forget using naan as a soft cushion on which to put torn pieces of mozzarella with tomatoes or an English muffin spread thick with hummus and fried mushrooms.

There are no rules really. The toast should be thick enough to support whatever we put on top of it and it should be hot and freshly made. Other than that, we are surely free to mix and match toasts and toppings at will. Authenticity is of little interest here; what matters is that the toast and partner are compatible.

A slice of toasted bread has the ability to make anything more substantial. A lump of cool, milky burrata with a trickle of peppery olive oil; a trio of roasted tomatoes, their skins blackened from the oven and scented with basil and butter; a spoon or three of last night's stew, brought to a steaming simmer; or the bread, cut thick and toasted and dunked into a bowl of soup, where it will slowly sponge up every bit of goodness and savor.

BEET, APPLE, GOAT CHEESE

Hot toast, cool cheese, crisp seeds.

Serves 2

pickled beet 3½ oz/100g
a small, sharp apple
cider vinegar 2 tablespoons
sunflower seeds 2 tablespoons
poppy seeds 2 tablespoons

rye or sourdough bread
　2 thick slices
goat cheese 7 oz/200g
dill, chopped 2 tablespoons

Coarsely grate the beet into a medium mixing bowl. Grate the apple into the beet but don't mix them together. Sprinkle the cider vinegar over the apple and beet.

In a dry pan, toast the sunflower seeds for three or four minutes till golden and fragrant, then mix them with the poppy seeds. Toast the bread lightly on both sides.

Stir the goat cheese into the apple and beet, together with a little salt and half the seeds and chopped dill. Spread the apple and goat cheese onto the toasts in thick waves, scatter over the remaining seeds and dill, and eat immediately, while the toast is still hot.

• A light stir is all you need to mix the cheese with the apple and beet. Over-mixing will result in a rather pink covering for your toast.
• Instead of the goat cheese, try fromage frais.

CRUMPETS, CREAM CHEESE, SPINACH

The comfort of crumpets. The goodness of greens.

Serves 2

spinach 3½ oz/100g
tarragon, chopped 1 tablespoon
chives, chopped 1 tablespoon
parsley, chopped 2 tablespoons

green onion 1
cream cheese 7 oz/200g
crumpets 4

Wash the spinach, remove any thick stems, then pile the still-wet leaves into a saucepan. Place the pan over moderate heat, cover tightly with a lid, then let the leaves steam for a minute or two. Lift the lid and turn the leaves, so they soften evenly. When they are bright green and glossy, remove from the pan, squeeze the leaves almost dry, and chop roughly.

Mix the chopped tarragon, chives, and parsley together. Finely slice the green onion and mix with the herbs, then stir into the cream cheese. Season with black pepper and a little salt. Toast the crumpets till golden, then spread each generously with some of the herb cream cheese. Pile some of the spinach leaves on top and tuck in.

• The crumpet's holes have the ability to soak up anything we spread it with, from butter to herbed cream cheese. Rather than sit on top of the toasted crust, the melted cheese, cream, Marmite, or whatever trickles down through the holes to become part of the crumpet itself. An utterly joyous conception and the reason for keeping a package in the freezer.
• Once a crumpet is toasted, I find it best to cover the surface generously with something delicious, then return it briefly to the broiler. Crumpets don't hold the heat well, so an extra minute or so under the heat will ensure they are piping hot. *(continued)*

• A few delicious cheese-based ideas for your crumpets: butter and grated farmhouse cheeses; slices of soft Brie-type cheese and sharp fruit chutney such as apple or apricot; a spread made from equal amounts of butter and grated parmesan; cream cheese flecked with dill and chopped pickled cucumber; cream into which you have melted Taleggio and added a few thyme leaves; crème fraîche and black cherry jam.

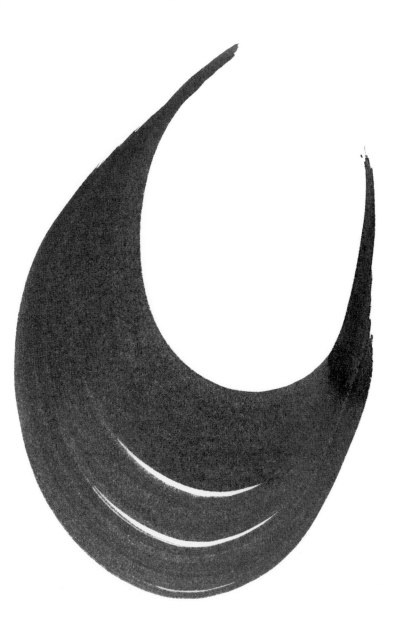

EGGS, SPINACH, BREAD

Spiced, eggy toasts.

Serves 2

spinach 7 oz/200g
curry powder 1 teaspoon
ground turmeric 1 teaspoon
ground cumin ½ teaspoon

dried chile flakes 1 teaspoon
eggs 4
ciabatta 4 thick slices
butter 3 tablespoons

Wash the spinach leaves, then put them, still very wet, into a deep saucepan with a tight-fitting lid. Place over high heat and let the spinach steam, turning it from time to time, until the leaves are dark green and wilted, a matter of five minutes or less. Remove the spinach from the pan, squeeze the leaves to remove most of the water, then chop finely.

Put the curry powder, turmeric, cumin, and chile flakes in a dry, shallow pan and toast over moderate heat for a minute or two till fragrant. Tip them into a medium mixing bowl, then break the eggs into the bowl, add a half teaspoon of salt, stir in the spinach leaves, and beat lightly to combine whites, yolks, spinach, and toasted spices.

Dunk the slices of ciabatta in the spiced batter, making sure they are well saturated. Melt the butter in a shallow pan, either nonstick or one with a good patina. As the butter warms, lower the bread into the pan, moderating the heat so it browns lightly on the base, making sure the butter doesn't burn — a matter of three or four minutes. Turn with an offset spatula and brown the other side. Drain lightly on a paper towel before eating.

• A substantial snack more than a meal, but a useful recipe to have on hand. Use any soft bread, preferably of the airy and light sort. I have known these to be made for breakfast on a Sunday morning, an occasion to which they seem most fitting. *(continued)*

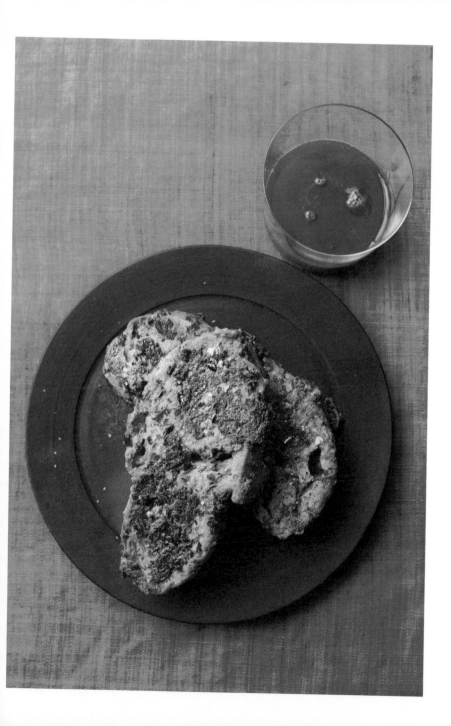

• Use your favorite curry powder or your own masala. You may have your own recipe or maybe a commercial brand, but either way add more or less to suit your taste.

LEEKS, CAERPHILLY, MUSTARD

The sweetness of leeks in butter. The quiet heat of mustard.

Serves 2

a large leek
butter 2 tablespoons
all-purpose flour 1 heaped
   tablespoon
heavy cream 1 cup/240ml

Caerphilly cheese 3½ oz/100g
grain mustard 1 tablespoon
Dijon mustard 1 tablespoon
crumpets, store bought 4

Thinly slice the leek, discarding any particularly thick, dark green leaves, and wash thoroughly. Put the still-wet leek in a deep saucepan over low heat with the butter and cover with a lid. Cook, with the occasional stir, for ten to fifteen minutes until they are softened. Don't let the leeks brown.

Stir the flour into the leeks, continue cooking for a couple of minutes, then pour in the cream. Coarsely grate the Caerphilly into the leeks, then season with the grain and smooth mustards and a little salt and black pepper.

Heat an overhead broiler. Toast the crumpets. Spoon the leek and cheese mixture over them and return to the broiler. Cook until the surface is patchily golden. (I like mine blistered dark brown here and there.)

• Onions make a sound substitute for the leeks. Onions take longer to cook, so fry them over low to moderate heat, stirring regularly, for a good thirty to forty minutes until they are deep golden brown.
• You can use a more strongly flavored cheese if you wish, even a blue variety such as Shropshire Blue or Stichelton, in which case I would forgo the mustards and add a spoonful more cream.

MUSHROOMS, BLUE CHEESE, ENGLISH MUFFINS

Toasted dough. Golden fungi. A savory butter.

Serves 2

brown button mushrooms,
    small 5¼ oz/150g
soft blue cheese such as
    Dolcelatte 1¾ oz/50g
butter 2 tablespoons

garlic 2 cloves
olive oil ¼ cup/60ml
thyme leaves 2 teaspoons
the juice of half a lemon
English muffins 2

Thinly slice the mushrooms. Cream together the blue cheese and butter. Peel and thinly slice the garlic.

Warm the olive oil in a shallow pan, add the garlic and let it soften. Add the mushrooms to the pan, followed by the thyme, and fry for six or seven minutes till they and the garlic are golden. Grind a little black pepper and squeeze the lemon juice over the mushrooms.

Split the muffins horizontally, toast them, then spread with the blue cheese butter. Pile the mushrooms on top and eat.

NAAN, MOZZARELLA, TOMATOES

Crisp dough. Soft cheese. Sweet-sharp tomatoes.

Serves 2

mozzarella 4½ oz/125g
feta 3½ oz/100g
cherry tomatoes 5¼ oz/150g

green onions 3
naan 2
cilantro leaves a handful

Set the oven at 450°F/220°C.

Coarsely grate the mozzarella into a bowl, then crumble the feta into it. Cut the tomatoes into quarters and roughly slice the green onions. Mix everything together and grind in a little black pepper.

Place the naan on a baking sheet and divide the tomato, mozzarella, and feta mixture between them. Bake for twelve minutes, or until the naan is crisp and the cheese is pale gold in patches. Scatter with cilantro leaves.

• Naan provides a generously sized base for anything you might usually put on a pizza. More interesting than most commercially made pizza bases, the best naan are lighter and fluffier and will crisp splendidly in the oven with their cargo of melting cheese.

• I love the cultural mix here of warm Indian dough with an Italian topping. Mozzarella provides a pool of molten cheese, to which you can add something more strongly flavored, such as parmesan or Pecorino, or a mixture of cheeses you wish to use up.

IN THE OVEN

A black, wet, winter's night. The kitchen is dark save for the light from the oven. A light as sweet as molasses. In the oven is a wedge of pumpkin or a humble baked potato, a roasting cauliflower or golden roots (parsnip, carrot, sweet potato) whose edges are slowly browning. There may be the scent of warm thyme or garlic. The burnt-sugar-and-butter smell of roasting onions or the resinous notes of rosemary twigs baking. Your oven may be home to a wide earthenware dish of sweet potato and cream, its edges bubbling and caramelizing in the heat. Or it could just be witness to a single baked potato, snowflakes of sea salt on its crisping skin, its insides slowly turning to a floury butter-yellow fluff.

My oven gets twice the use in winter it does during the other seasons. Occasionally I will slide a potato or more often a sweet potato on the bottom shelf and leave it to bake while I make a salad — of watercress and fennel or red treviso and oakleaf lettuce. Winter salad leaves are crisp, bitter, and pale (chicory, Castelfranco, frisée), and benefit from citrus notes of orange and grapefruit, of toasted nuts warm from the pan, and from dressing spiked with mustard, grated horseradish, or ginger.

I like the thought that while baking or roasting, no flavor has the chance to escape, every bit of it trapped by the walls of the oven. In reality, a crust forms on top of the food rather than underneath, as it does with food cooked on the stove — a crust that seems to seal in flavor. But these of course are the romantic notions of a hungry cook, not those of the scientist. I know which I would rather be.

There is an ease to food that is baked or roasted. The oven does much of the work for us. There is no moving food around the pan, turning or stirring. No tinkering with the heat. That said, it is often a good idea to baste something as it cooks — spoon a pumpkin with the butter that has melted around it; douse a mushroom with the pool of olive oil and spices it's cooking in.

The dish in which you bake or roast matters little as long as it is strong enough not to buckle in the heat. You can bake in an aluminum tray if you have to. In my experience, the thinner the pan, the more likely the contents are to burn. Deep-sided dishes are good for baking, less so for roasting. Vegetables cooked in a deep-sided dish are less likely to toast and brown, as they tend to produce steam. To get a good toasted crust all round, roast in a shallow-sided pan.

The one oven-based supper to which I return time and again is that of simple roasted vegetables: peeled parsnips or sliced eggplants, onions, or red peppers that you have tossed in olive oil and butter, salt, pepper, and herbs and roasted at a high temperature till the edges are sweet and dark. I let them cool, then dress them with their caramelized cooking juices and a squeeze of lemon or some red wine vinegar. I eat them on their own or with a mash of canned beans or a ladleful of pale golden polenta, or trickle them with a dressing of tahini and yogurt. Opening the fridge on a winter's night and finding a dish of yesterday's roast vegetables is as good as an impromptu supper gets. So make twice as much as you need, leaving some to come home to tomorrow.

ARTICHOKES, WINTER ROOTS, SMOKED SALT

Deep drifts of mash. Toasted, smoky vegetables.

Serves 4
For the mash:
celery root 1 lb 10 oz/750g
Jerusalem artichokes 9 oz/250g
butter ¼ cup/50g
hot vegetable or chicken stock
   1 cup/240ml

For the roast roots:
carrots, small to medium 8

parsnips 2
garlic 6 cloves
beets, small raw 4
thyme 8 sprigs
butter 5 tablespoons/75g
sunflower seeds 3 tablespoons
parsley, chopped 2 heaped
   tablespoons
smoked salt 2 teaspoons

Set the oven at 425°F/200°C. Peel the celery root and cut into large pieces about the size of roasted potatoes. Put them in a roasting pan. Peel the artichokes, then add them to the roasting pan. Break the butter into small pieces and dot over the vegetables, season with salt, then roast for about an hour until lightly browned. They mustn't crisp like roast potatoes, but instead develop pale gold, lightly caramelized edges. Test them for softness; a skewer should slide through them with ease. Set aside to cool, and wipe out the roasting pan.

Scrub or peel the carrots as you wish, then cut them in half lengthwise. Do the same with the parsnips, peeling them if their skins are tough (as they often can be) and cutting them in half. Put the carrots and parsnips in the roasting pan. Tuck the garlic cloves, still in their skins, among the carrots. Trim the little beets, cut into quarters, then add to the pan along with the sprigs of thyme and the butter. Season generously, then bake for about an hour. Turn the vegetables over once or twice as they roast.

Tip the roast celery root and artichokes into a food processor, add most of the stock and blend to a smooth purée, introducing more of the

(continued)

stock as necessary. Check the seasoning, adding more salt and pepper as you wish. In a small pan, toast the sunflower seeds over high heat till they smell nutty, then mix with the chopped parsley and smoked salt.

Spoon the mash onto a serving dish, add the roast vegetables, scatter with the seeds and parsley, and serve.

BRUSSELS SPROUTS, SMOKED MOZZARELLA, DILL

Greens, herbs, and cream.

Serves 3
Brussels sprouts 10½ oz/300g
butter 3 tablespoons
olive oil 2 tablespoons
dill, chopped ¾ cup/15g
smoked mozzarella 9 oz/250g
heavy cream 1 cup/240ml

For the crumbs:
butter 3 tablespoons
coarse breadcrumbs a handful
dill, chopped 3 tablespoons

Set the oven at 425°F/200°C. Trim and shred the Brussels sprouts. Warm the butter and olive oil in a shallow pan, then add the sprouts and cook for two minutes until they brighten in color. Fold in the chopped dill, a little salt, and a grind or two of black pepper. Cut the smoked mozzarella into thick slices.

Put half the sprouts into a baking dish, place most of the mozzarella among them, then a second layer of sprouts, finishing with the remaining cheese.

Make the crumbs: warm the butter in a shallow pan, add the crumbs and cook till golden, then stir in the chopped dill. Pour the cream over the sprouts and cheese, scatter with the crumbs and dill, and bake for twenty-five minutes or until bubbling.

• A dish to warm the soul. You could use shredded cabbage, cauliflower, or lightly cooked kale in place of the sprouts. The mozzarella could be replaced by a blue cheese of some sort, which would flatter the greens.
• Should you have any leftover cooked pasta, you could incorporate it with the sprouts and cheese.

LIMA BEANS, PEPPERS, EGGPLANTS

Clouds of mash. Sweet, sharp juices.

Serves 4

small red peppers 14 oz/400g
cherry tomatoes 9 oz/250g
small eggplants 14 oz/400g
garlic 6 fat cloves
rosemary 3 large sprigs
olive oil 5 tablespoons/75ml
lima beans 1 × 23-oz/650g jar or
  2 × 15-oz/400g cans

Set the oven at 425°F/200°C. Place the whole peppers, cherry tomatoes, and eggplants in a roasting pan. Tuck the garlic cloves, still in their skins, and the rosemary among the vegetables, then drizzle with the olive oil. Let the vegetables roast in the preheated oven for thirty to forty minutes, until they are approaching softness, then push them to one side of the roasting pan. Drain the lima beans and tip them into the pan. Stir the beans to coat them in oil and roasting juices, then return to the oven and cook for another twenty minutes until all is soft and golden.

Remove the garlic from the roasting pan and squeeze each clove from its skin into the bowl of a food processor. Tip in the warm beans and process to a thick, fluffy purée. Check the seasoning, then pile the purée onto a serving plate and place the vegetables on top. Spoon any juices over the vegetables.

• If you can track down the large, flat Judión beans in jars, then I recommend them for this. They are particularly soft and buttery and produce a cloudlike mash. Canned lima beans work well enough, are cheap, and are easier to locate. You may like to add a thick slice of butter as you blend them. The vegetables can be roasted ahead of time and served warm or even cold, but the beans must be blended while they are still warm, if you are to achieve a smooth finish. *(continued)*

• Once the weather cools and summer slides toward autumn, you could roast slices of orange-fleshed squash instead of the eggplants or use parsnips in place of the lima beans. The real point of the dish is the sweet, herb-infused roasting juices trickling into the cloud of mash.

CABBAGE, BERBERE SPICE, CRUMBS

Toasted cabbage. Crisp crumbs. Green peas.

Serves 2

cabbage 10½ oz/300g
olive oil 12 tablespoons/180ml
fresh white breadcrumbs
    1 cup/80g

Berbere spice mix 1 teaspoon
frozen peas ⅔ cup/100g
mint leaves 12

Set the oven at 425°F/200°C. Slice the cabbage into ¾-inch/2cm-thick pieces and put them on a foil-lined baking sheet. Trickle over six tablespoons of the oil and bake for twenty-five minutes.

Warm three tablespoons of the oil in a shallow pan, add the crumbs and toast them till golden, tossing them from time to time. Stir in the Berbere spice mix.

In a food processor, blend the peas with the remaining oil and the mint leaves until lightly chopped. Stir into the warm crumbs and let the peas thaw in the residual heat. Remove the cabbage from the oven, slide onto plates with a fish spatula or offset spatula, then scatter with the peas and crumbs.

• A crisp, rock-hard white cabbage is probably more suitable for roasting than an open-leaved dark green Savoy, which tends to cook to a crisp too easily.

• This recipe works with Brussels sprouts too. Slice them thickly and lay them out on the baking sheet. The result will be messier to serve, but will taste just as good.

• Berbere spice mixes are available from any major supermarket or specialty grocers. The mix is sweet and warm rather than hot and usually contains chile, cumin, ginger, cardamom, nutmeg, and fenugreek. Good for adding to melted butter and tossing with steamed long-grain rice or couscous.

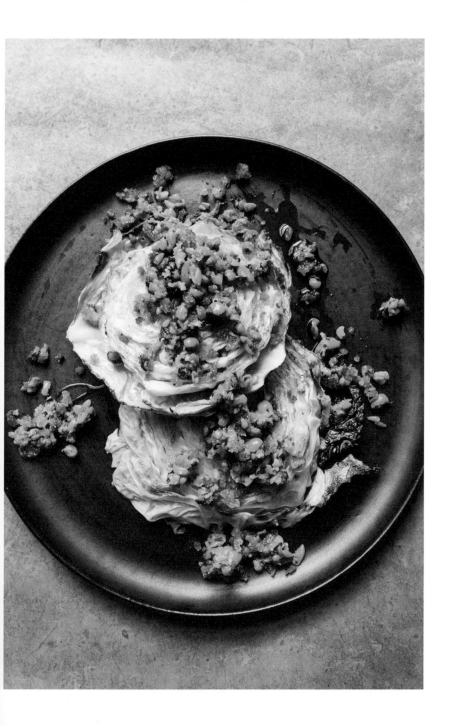

CARROTS, SPICES, PANEER

Sweet vegetables. Earthy spice.

Serves 2–4

small carrots, assorted colors and sizes 1 lb 12 oz/800g
peanut oil 5 tablespoons/75ml
coriander seeds 1 teaspoon
cumin seeds 1 teaspoon
nigella seeds 1 teaspoon
black mustard seeds 1 teaspoon
paneer 9 oz/250g

Set the oven at 425°F/200°C. Trim and scrub the carrots and put them in a large roasting pan. Pour in the oil and toss gently to coat. Roast for forty to forty-five minutes till tender, tossing them halfway through.

Warm the coriander, cumin, nigella, and mustard seeds in a dry pan for a couple of minutes. As soon as the spices smell toasted and are starting to pop, crush them coarsely using a mortar and pestle, or give them a brief ride in a spice mill. Scatter the spices over the carrots with a little salt and toss gently, then remove the carrots from their pan and transfer to a serving dish.

Place the pan over moderate heat and add the paneer, crumbling it as you go. Let the paneer fry, with the occasional turn, until it is golden. Scatter the paneer over the carrots and serve.

• If paneer isn't your thing, it is well worth making this with feta cheese or halloumi instead. I have also brought these roasted, spiced vegetables out with soft, fresh goat cheese to add in cloudlike mounds at the table.
• Parsnips, cut into thin lengths, can work here too, and take this particular spicing well.

CAULIFLOWER, ONIONS, BAY

Cloves, green onions, and bay. Flavors to soothe.

Serves 4

a cauliflower, about 2 lb 2 oz/1kg
olive oil 6 tablespoons/90ml
white onions, large 2
butter 5 tablespoons/75g
milk 2 cups/480ml

bay leaves 3
cloves 3
black peppercorns 8
green onions 4

Set the oven at 425°F/200°C. Trim the cauliflower, removing any imperfect or tough leaves, keeping any small, young ones in place. Put the cauliflower stem down in a roasting pan, pour five tablespoons of the olive oil over the top, and season with sea salt and ground black pepper. When the oven is up to heat, roast the cauliflower for fifty minutes to an hour, or until the florets are golden brown. Check its tenderness with a metal skewer — it should go through the thickest part of the cauliflower with ease.

While the cauliflower roasts, make the sauce. Peel and roughly chop the white onions. Warm the remaining olive oil and the butter in a deep pan over gentle heat, add the onions and let them cook, covered by a lid, till soft and translucent. Let them take their time — they need a good twenty-five minutes — and stir them regularly, so they do not color.

Pour the milk over the softened onions, add the bay leaves, cloves, and peppercorns, and bring to a boil. Remove the pan from the heat and cover, allowing the milk to infuse for forty minutes.

Remove the bay, peppercorns, and cloves, then use an immersion blender to blend to a smooth and creamy sauce (or, better, I think, use a countertop blender). Season carefully, then finely chop the green onions. Return the onion sauce to its pan, stir in the green onions, and warm over moderate heat, stirring almost continuously, till hot. Transfer the cauliflower to a serving dish. Pour the onion sauce on top and serve.

CHEDDAR, TARRAGON, EGGS

Light, airy. A cheese and tarragon soufflé.

Serves 2

To prepare the dish:
a knob of butter
parmesan, finely grated
   1 tablespoon

For the souffle:
milk 1¼ cups/300ml
a bay leaf
a small onion, peeled
butter ¼ cup/55g

all-purpose flour
   6 tablespoons/50g
eggs, large 4, separated
strongly flavored firm cheese,
   such as Yarg, Gruyère,
   cheddar, grated or cut into
   small pieces 3½ oz/100g
tarragon leaves, chopped
   2 tablespoons
parmesan, grated 1 tablespoon

Lightly butter the inside of a deep soufflé or similar dish measuring 8 inches/20cm across the top. Scatter in the grated parmesan, tipping the dish from side to side to make sure the cheese sticks to the butter.

Put a baking sheet in the oven and set at 425°F/200°C. Bring the milk to a boil in a small pan together with the bay leaf and peeled onion. Turn off the heat and let it sit for a few minutes.

Melt the butter in a small, heavy-bottomed saucepan, stir in the flour, and cook over the heat for two or three minutes, stirring almost continuously. Stir in the warm milk, gradually at first (you can chuck the bay and onion at this point — they have done their work), then a little faster, till you have a thick sauce. Let it come to an enthusiastic bubble, then lower the heat and let the mixture simmer for at least five minutes, until it thickens.

If your sauce looks lumpy, whisk it fiercely until it is smooth. Remove from the heat, cool briefly, then stir or whisk in the egg yolks, one at a time. Work quickly, otherwise the egg will cook before it gets stirred in.

(continued)

Stir in the grated cheese and the chopped tarragon. In a large bowl and using a large whisk, beat the egg whites till stiff and frothy. Fold them gently but firmly into the cheese sauce, then immediately scrape into the buttered dish.

Smooth the top lightly, scatter with the grated parmesan, then place on top of the hot baking sheet and bake for twenty to twenty-five minutes.

To test if your soufflé is done, push the dish firmly with your oven mitt: it should shudder but not wobble violently. The crust should be pale to mid-brown, the center should be soft and oozing. Remove and serve immediately. If you stick your spoon in and the middle is too liquid, put it back in the oven. It will still rise.

• The cheese is up to you. This can be a good way of using up bits you have lurking in the fridge. However, the flavor is best when the cheese has a good, strong character. Waxy budget cheese doesn't have the clout — a strong farmhouse cheese with some bite to it is what you need.

CHEESE, THYME, GRAPES

Molten, oozing cheese. Cold sweet grapes.

Serves 2

a whole small Camembert or
    Tunworth cheese, preferably
    one in a wooden box
thyme 4 sprigs

black peppercorns 6
olive oil 2 tablespoons
crusty bread, to serve
grapes, to serve

Set the oven at 425°F/200°C. Remove the cheese from its waxed paper and return it to the little wooden box. Wrap the underside and edges of the box tightly with foil to prevent the cheese from leaking. Put the thyme sprigs and peppercorns on the surface of the cheese and moisten them with the olive oil.

Bake for twenty minutes, or until the cheese is molten inside. Serve with bread, preferably with a good crisp crust, and some sweet black grapes.

• Check that the wooden box the cheese comes in is stapled, not glued. If glued then it is inclined to come undone in the oven and your liquid cheese will escape.
• I sometimes add half a dozen juniper berries, lightly crushed, to the surface of the cheese as well.

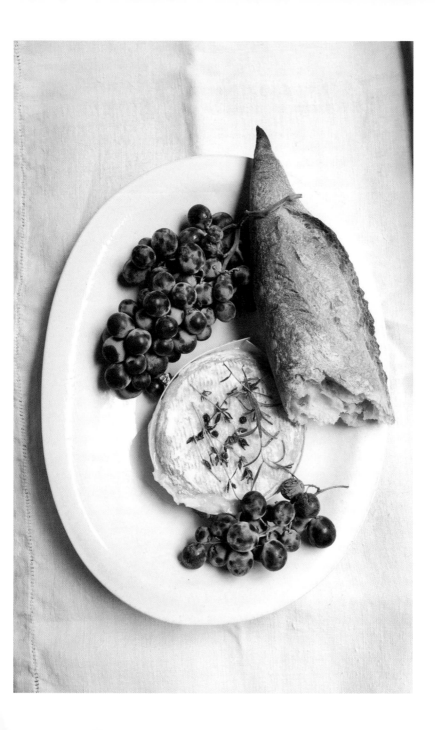

CHICKPEAS, RADICCHIO, LIMA BEANS

Soft, floury beans and chickpeas. The sweet juice of roasted lemon.

Serves 2

chickpeas 1 × 15-oz/400g can
shallots, medium 6
olive oil ¼ cup/60ml
a lemon
thyme 6 bushy sprigs

lima beans 1 × 15-oz/400g can
tahini 2 teaspoons
a small orange
radicchio or red chicory
14 oz/400g

Set the oven at 425°F/200°C. Drain the chickpeas in a sieve. Peel the shallots, halve them lengthwise and put them into a roasting dish, cut side down. Tip the chickpeas into the roasting pan, trickle with the olive oil, and grind a little black pepper and salt over the top.

Cut the lemon in half, squeeze lightly over the shallots, then tuck the lemon halves into the pan. Pick the thyme leaves from their stems, scatter them over the chickpeas and shallots, then roast for about thirty minutes, until the shallots are soft and their undersides are golden.

Lift the roasting pan onto the stove and transfer the shallots to a serving dish, leaving the chickpeas in the pan. Place the pan over moderate heat and tip in the lima beans, drained of their canning liquor. Squeeze the roasted lemons over the beans and chickpeas, then stir in the tahini and the juice of the orange.

Continue cooking until all is hot, then return the shallots to the roasting pan, tear the radicchio leaves into large pieces, and fold everything together before transferring to a serving dish.

• It is useful to have a stash of roasted chickpeas around. You can make them and set them aside for a day or two, to be used as you wish: tossed as above with bitter leaves and citrus, folded into a salad of young spinach leaves, or piled onto thick olive-oily toast.

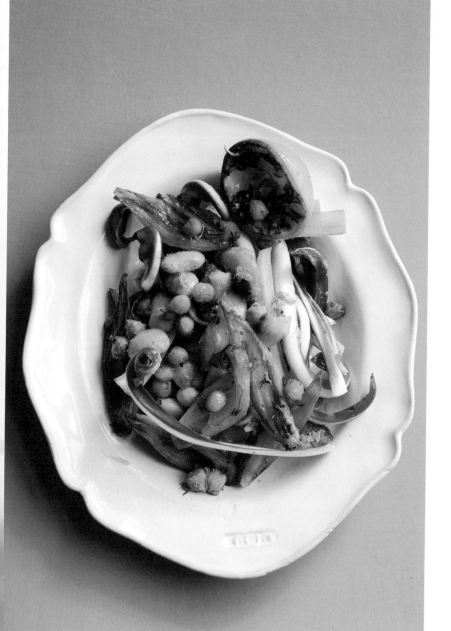

FENNEL, CREAM, PINE NUTS

Aniseed, citrus, crumbs, and cream.

Serves 2

fennel 1 lb 10 oz/750g
olive oil
heavy cream 1 cup/240ml
fresh white bread 1½ oz/45g

parsley leaves ½ cup/10g
zest of 1 orange, finely grated
pine nuts ¼ cup/25g

Set the oven at 425°F/200°C. Trim the fennel, then slice into pieces no thicker than a pencil. The thicker you slice them, the longer they will take to cook. Warm a thin layer of olive oil in an ovenproof frying pan, then add the fennel, a few pieces at a time if there isn't room for them all at once, and let them cook until pale gold. Remove from the heat and pour in the cream.

Tear up the white bread and place in the bowl of a food processor. Add the parsley leaves, the grated zest of the orange, a little salt and black pepper, and the pine nuts. Process briefly to create a rough-textured crumb mixture.

Scatter the seasoned breadcrumb mixture over the surface of the cream. Trickle a little olive oil over the crumbs. Bake for twenty to twenty-five minutes until the cream is bubbling around the edges.

• Cooking fennel in this way softens the vegetable's aniseed notes. You can also make this recipe with celery instead of fennel, cutting the ribs into short lengths and baking with the cream as above.
• I sometimes bake small, floury potatoes at the same time, then spoon the fennel cream over the baked potato, mashing the aniseed-scented cream into the soft flesh of the potato.

LENTILS, SWEET POTATO, TOMATOES

A deep dish of comfort.

Serves 4

split yellow lentils 1⅓ cups/250g
ground turmeric 1 teaspoon
vegetable stock 3¼ cups/750ml
sweet potatoes 1 lb 10 oz/750g
onion 1
olive oil 2 tablespoons
ginger 2¼ oz/60g
garlic 2 cloves
cumin seeds ½ teaspoon

green cardamom pods 10
chile flakes ½ teaspoon
curry leaves 12
ground cayenne 1½ teaspoons
chopped tomatoes 1 × 15-oz/
   400g can
a little melted butter or oil,
   for baking

Wash the lentils in cold water, until the water is no longer milky. Tip them into a medium saucepan, add the turmeric and stock, and bring to a boil. Lower the heat, partially cover with a lid, and simmer for ten minutes, until most of the stock has been absorbed and the lentils are almost tender.

Peel the sweet potatoes and cut them into slices about one-quarter inch/half a centimeter in thickness. Put them in a steamer basket or colander over a pan of boiling water, and cover. Steam for seven to eight minutes until soft to the point of a knife. Remove the pan from the heat.

Peel and roughly chop the onion. Warm the oil in a deep pan over moderate heat, add the onion, and cook until it is soft and pale gold — a matter of twenty minutes. Peel and grate the ginger. Peel and finely slice the garlic, then stir into the onion with the ginger and cumin seeds. Continue cooking for two or three minutes. Crack open the cardamom pods, extract the seeds, grind to a coarse powder, then stir into the onion together with the chile flakes, curry leaves, and ground cayenne. Add

(continued)

pepper and half a teaspoon of salt, stirring for a minute or two. Set the oven at 425°F/200°C.

Put the lentils over moderate heat, stir in the tomatoes, then mix in the onion and remove from the heat.

Carefully lift the sweet potatoes from the steamer with an offset spatula. Using a baking dish measuring approximately 10 inches/25cm, place half the lentil mixture in the base, then add half the sweet potatoes over the surface, followed by a second layer of lentils and then the remaining sweet potatoes. Brush with butter or oil. Bake for thirty to forty minutes until bubbling around the edges and lightly browned on top.

• One of those dishes that is somehow even better the next day, when slowly reheated in a moderate oven.

MUSHROOMS, CHICKPEAS, TAHINI

A mushroom as thick as a steak. A silky purée.

Serves 2

large portobello mushrooms 2
olive oil 8 tablespoons/120ml
garlic 2 cloves, peeled
ground sumac 2 teaspoons
juice of half a lemon

chickpeas 1 × 15-oz/400g can
tahini 2 tablespoons
thyme leaves 1 tablespoon
black sesame seeds 1 tablespoon
white sesame seeds 1 tablespoon

Set the oven at 425°F/200°C. Cut out the stalks from the mushrooms, then place the mushrooms gill side up on a baking sheet. Score the inside of each mushroom with the tip of a knife — this will allow the oil to penetrate — then pour one tablespoon of olive oil into each.

Use a mortar and pestle to crush the garlic, then pound in four tablespoons of the olive oil, the sumac, lemon juice, and a little salt. Drain the chickpeas, then mash half into the oil and garlic paste. Stir in the tahini, thyme leaves, and half of both the sesame seeds.

Fill the mushrooms with the chickpea paste, then cover each with the reserved whole chickpeas. Finally, trickle with the last of the olive oil and scatter with the reserved sesame seeds. Bake for about thirty minutes.

• The best mushrooms for these are the very large portobello mushrooms with upturned edges to hold the filling.

ONIONS, TALEGGIO, CREAM

Caramelized onions. Melting cheese.

Serves 4

onions, medium 8
bay leaves 3
black peppercorns 12
olive oil 3 tablespoons

butter ¼ cup/60g
thyme 8 sprigs
heavy cream 1 cup/240ml
Taleggio 7 oz/200g

Bring a large, deep pot of water to a boil. Set the oven at 425°F/200°C. Peel the onions, keeping them whole. Add the bay leaves and peppercorns to the boiling water, then lower in the peeled onions. Cook the onions at a brisk simmer for about thirty minutes, till they are soft and yielding.

Lift the onions out with a slotted spoon and put them into a baking dish. Pour the olive oil over the onions, add the butter, the leaves from half the thyme sprigs, and a little black pepper, then bake for about thirty minutes, basting once or twice as they cook.

Warm the cream in a small saucepan over low heat. Cut the Taleggio into small pieces, then allow to melt in the cream, without stirring, adding the remaining sprigs of thyme.

Serve two onions per person, together with some of the Taleggio and thyme sauce.

• I sometimes serve this with a tangle of boiled noodles, or a spoonful of gnocchi, to stir into the cheese sauce. The onions and their sauce are wonderful on thick slices of sourdough toast too.

PARSNIPS, SHALLOTS, GOAT CHEESE

Sweet, crisp, and chewy parsnips. Thick and glossy gravy.

Serves 4

parsnips, medium 6
olive oil ⅔ cup/160ml
rosemary 6 sprigs
dried porcini ½ oz/15g

large shallots 4
all-purpose flour 2 tablespoons
thyme 10 sprigs
goat cheese 3½ oz/100g

Set the oven at 425°F/200°C. Peel the parsnips, cut them in half length-wise, then in half again. Put them into a roasting pan with seven tablespoons/100ml of the olive oil, the rosemary, and a little salt and black pepper. Let the parsnips roast for an hour, turning them halfway through.

Bring a quart/liter of water to a boil in a deep saucepan. Add the porcini, cover with a lid, and continue cooking on very low heat for twenty minutes.

Peel the shallots and cut them into thick slices. In a large pan, cook them in the remaining oil for fifteen to twenty minutes over moderate heat till soft. As they turn translucent and pale gold, add the flour and continue to cook, stirring regularly, for three minutes.

Pour the porcini and their broth into the shallots, a little at a time, stirring almost continuously. Remove the leaves from the thyme and stir in. Turn up the heat and let the sauce bubble for five minutes or so until you have a rich, quite thick gravy.

Remove the parsnips when they are golden and lightly crisp, spoon the shallot and porcini gravy on top, and serve with the goat cheese.

• The shallots need to cook until they are golden and you can crush them between your finger and thumb, but stop well before they become nut brown and caramelized. Sticky, pale gold, and translucent is perfect.

PARSNIPS, SMOKED GARLIC, FETA

Smoky, salty, sweet, and toasted.

Serves 2

red onions 2
rutabaga 1 lb 5 oz/600g
parsnips 2
carrots, medium 4
thyme 6 bushy sprigs

smoked garlic a whole head
olive oil 6 tablespoons/90ml
fennel seeds 1 teaspoon
yellow mustard seeds 1 teaspoon
feta 7 oz/200g

Set the oven at 425°F/200°C. Peel the red onions, cut them in half, then into thick segments. Peel and thickly slice the rutabaga, then cut each slice into pieces roughly 1½ inches/4cm long. Do the same with the parsnips. Scrub the carrots, then cut into thick pieces and mix with the onions, rutabaga, and parsnips in a large roasting pan.

Tuck the thyme and smoked garlic among the vegetables, then pour in the olive oil. Roast for twenty-five minutes, then turn the vegetables over in the roasting pan and cook for another twenty minutes. Remove the garlic from the roasting pan. Scatter the fennel and mustard seeds over the vegetables and return to the oven for another twenty minutes till all is sizzling and the vegetables are knife-point tender.

Squeeze the smoked garlic flesh from its papery skin, crush it to a paste with a mortar and pestle or a spoon, then crumble the feta into it. Remove the roasted vegetables from the oven, then toss gently with the garlic and feta.

• A fine way to utilize the rutabaga that turned up in the CSA box. You could use pretty much any root vegetables in this, including young turnips or celery root. If using the latter, make sure to baste regularly.

POTATOES, BRUSSELS SPROUTS

A cure for everything.

Serves 2

russet potatoes 4
garlic a whole head
heavy cream 1 cup/240ml

Brussels sprouts 10½ oz/300g
olive oil 3 tablespoons

Prick the skins of the potatoes here and there with a fork. Bake them for about an hour at 425°F/200°C, until their skins are crisp and the inside is fluffy. Put the garlic in the oven and roast for forty-five minutes, till the cloves are soft inside.

Remove the garlic from the oven, squeeze the cloves from their skins, and crush the flesh to a paste with a fork. Put it in a saucepan, pour in the cream, and bring to a boil, then remove from the heat.

Quarter the Brussels sprouts. Warm the oil in a shallow pan, add the sprouts, and let them brown lightly. Take the potatoes from the oven, slice off their tops and scoop the flesh into the pan with the sprouts. Fold the vegetables together, then stir in the warm garlic cream. Season with salt and black pepper, then spoon the filling back into the empty potato skins.

Return the potatoes to the oven for ten minutes, till piping hot.

• There isn't much I haven't stuffed into a baked potato in my time, from smoked mackerel and cream to crisp bacon and its fat. But a big fat potato responds to other vegetables too. Try spooning in greens that you have sautéed in olive oil and lemon, a purée of green peas and mint, fried mushrooms with garlic and butter and mint, or cauliflower cooked with cream and parmesan.
• The Brussels sprouts work well with a baked sweet potato too. They probably shouldn't, but the slight bitterness of the sprouts is surprisingly happy with the caramelized flesh of the sweet potato.

POTATOES, SWEET POTATOES, CREAM

The peace of potatoes and cream. The warm glow of spice.

Serves 4

butter 1½ tablespoons
onions, large 2
olive oil 5 tablespoons/75ml
russet potatoes 1 lb 2 oz/500g
sweet potatoes 1 lb 2 oz/500g

mild paprika 2 teaspoons
yellow mustard seeds
 2 teaspoons
chile flakes 2 teaspoons
heavy cream 3¼ cups/750ml

Lightly butter a shallow, ovenproof 12-inch/30cm dish. Set the oven at 350°F/160°C. Peel the onions and slice them into ½-inch/1cm-thick rings.

Warm the olive oil in a deep pot, add the onions and let them cook until golden and soft. Expect them to take a good twenty-five to thirty minutes, with the occasional stir.

Peel and cut the russet potatoes into ¼-inch/0.5cm-thick slices, then peel the sweet potatoes and cut them into slightly thicker slices, but no more than ½ inch/1cm.

When the onions are golden, add the paprika, mustard seeds, and chile flakes, a good grinding of salt and black pepper, and the cream and bring to a boil. Immediately remove from the heat.

Layer the potatoes of both varieties and the paprika cream in the buttered dish, then bake for an hour and a half until bubbling and golden.

• Dauphinoise, updated with sweet potatoes and a generous hit of spice. Some salad leaves are needed with this, I think — something crisp, like chicory and iceberg lettuce or frisée with watercress. A sharp or piquant dressing would be my first choice — I'm thinking of red wine vinegar, peppercorns in brine, capers, or something citrusy.

POTATOES, TAHINI, THYME

Roasties. Sesame. Lemon.

Serves 2

yellow fleshed potatoes
   1 lb 12 oz/800g
olive oil 5 tablespoons/75ml
thyme 8 sprigs
garlic cloves 2
fennel seeds 2 teaspoons
green onions 2

For the dressing:
juice of a lemon
tahini 1 tablespoon
olive oil as needed

Set the oven at 425°F/200°C. Cut the potatoes into 1-inch/2.5cm pieces. Boil them in salted water till just tender, about fifteen minutes.

Drain the potatoes, put them on a roasting pan or baking sheet with the olive oil, thyme sprigs, and unpeeled garlic and scatter with the fennel seeds. Turn the potatoes so they are coated, then roast for about fifty minutes until golden and crisp, removing the garlic after thirty.

Cut the green onions into 1¼-inch/3cm lengths and add to the roasting pan for the final ten minutes. Squeeze the garlic from its skin, then crush the soft golden flesh with the lemon juice and tahini. Stir in the oil from the roasting pan. Should the dressing need it, add a little more olive oil to bring it to a smooth, pourable consistency.

Divide the potatoes between plates and spoon on the tahini dressing.

• I have yet to finish a jar of tahini. I usually need a couple of tablespoons for a special recipe then don't use any more for weeks or even months. Finding an everyday recipe that uses it is something of a gift and may help with getting through an entire jar before its sell-by date.
• This is one of my favorite recipes in the book, and I would be happy to eat it as a main dish, with salad leaves on the side.

POTATOES, TOMATOES, HORSERADISH

"Toast-rack" potatoes, spicy tomato sauce.

Serves 3

potatoes, large 6
olive oil 6 tablespoons/90ml
tomatoes 1 lb 12 oz/800g

garlic 6 cloves
fresh horseradish, grated
6 tablespoons

Set the oven at 425°F/200°C. Place the potatoes flat on a chopping board, then slice them at ¼-inch/0.5cm intervals, cutting almost through to the wood. It becomes immediately obvious why they are sometimes called toast-rack potatoes.

Place the potatoes in a roasting pan, trickle with some of the olive oil, and roast for about forty-five minutes till crisp and golden. Meanwhile put the tomatoes and unpeeled garlic cloves in a small roasting pan with the remaining olive oil, grind a little salt and black pepper over them, then place in the oven. Roast the tomatoes for thirty-five to forty minutes, until they are soft and lightly browned.

Remove the tomatoes and garlic from the oven. Pop the garlic from its skin and add the flesh to the tomatoes. Crush the tomatoes and garlic with a fork, stirring in the fresh horseradish as you go. When the potatoes are crisp and golden, remove them from the oven and serve with spoonfuls of the crushed tomato.

• Some people find it easier to "hasselback" the potatoes by placing each one in the hollow of a wooden spoon and slicing downward, thus avoiding cutting through to the chopping board. It's a good trick.

PUMPKIN, CHICKPEAS, ROSEMARY

Roasted pumpkin. Smooth, silky mash.

Serves 4

pumpkin, skin on 2 lb 2 oz/1kg
garlic 4 cloves
rosemary 10 sprigs
thyme 8 bushy sprigs
a little olive oil
butter 5 tablespoons/75g

For the hummus:

chickpeas 2 × 15-oz/400g cans
juice of a small lemon
olive oil ½ cup plus
        2 tablespoons/150ml
parsley leaves ½ cup/10g
pink peppercorns 2 teaspoons

Set the oven at 425°F/200°C. Remove the seeds and fibers from the pumpkin, then cut the flesh into eight wedges. Lightly oil a baking pan (I like to line mine with aluminum foil for easier cleaning) and lay the wedges down in a single layer. Tuck in the unpeeled garlic cloves. Season with salt, black pepper, and the sprigs of herbs, then moisten with olive oil. Dot the butter in small lumps over the pumpkin and roast for forty-five minutes, until the squash is golden brown in color and the texture is soft and fudgy.

Drain the chickpeas and bring them to a boil in deep water. Turn the heat down a little and let them simmer for eight to ten minutes till thoroughly hot. Squeeze the roast garlic cloves out of their skins. Drain the chickpeas again, then tip them into the bowl of a food processor. Add the lemon juice and garlic and process, pouring in enough of the oil (about ½ cup) to produce a soft, spreadable cream.

Chop the parsley and peppercorns together, then moisten with a tablespoon of olive oil. Spoon the hummus onto a serving dish, place the roasted pumpkin pieces on top, then scatter with the parsley and peppercorns and serve. *(continued)*

• If you don't have pink peppercorns (they are hardly a kitchen essential), then I can recommend those dark green bottled peppercorns instead. They have both warmth and piquancy and are useful as a seasoning for anything containing beans or cheese. The brine they come in is handy, too. Just a few drops will perk up a salad dressing or a vegetable or bean purée.

PUMPKIN, COUSCOUS, DATE SYRUP

Sweet, fudgy flesh. Tart, bright dressing.

Serves 4

pumpkin 2 lb 2 oz/1kg
olive oil ¼ cup/60ml
za'atar 1 tablespoon
dried chile flakes 1 teaspoon
couscous ⅓ cup/65g
cilantro 1 cup/20g
parsley leaves ½ cup/10g

For the dressing:

garlic 1 clove
date syrup 4 teaspoons
olive oil 5 tablespoons/75ml
juice of half a lemon
grain mustard 1 teaspoon

Set the oven at 425°F/200°C. Peel the pumpkin, remove and discard the fibers and seeds, then cut the flesh into ¾-inch/2cm-thick slices. Place the slices on a baking sheet. Mix together the olive oil, za'atar, and chile flakes, then spoon on the pumpkin. Bake for thirty-five to forty minutes till tender and translucent.

Bring a kettle of water to a boil. Put the couscous in a heatproof bowl, pour in enough of the hot water to cover, and set aside.

Make the dressing: crush the garlic and mix with the date syrup, olive oil, lemon juice, and grain mustard. Chop the cilantro and the parsley.

When the couscous has soaked up the water, separate the grains with a fork, then fold in the parsley and cilantro and season with salt and pepper. Remove the pumpkin from the oven, place the couscous on a serving plate with the pumpkin, then trickle the dressing over the top.

• Butternut squash is a handy year-round alternative to pumpkin and can be substituted here with ease. Butternut usually takes slightly less time than a variety such as Crown Prince, with its dense flesh. The trick as always with members of the squash family is to cook them until the golden interior is almost translucent and easily crushable with the back of a spoon.

PUMPKIN, MUSTARD, CREAM

Soft squash. The warmth of mustard.

Serves 3

pumpkin, skin on 4 lb 8 oz/2kg
olive oil 4 tablespoons/60ml
chicken or vegetable stock, hot,
   1 quart/1 liter
heavy cream ¾ cup plus
   2 tablespoons/200ml

grain mustard 1 tablespoon
smooth Dijon mustard
   1 tablespoon

Cut the pumpkin in half and each half into three large wedges. Remove and discard the seeds and fibers. Warm the olive oil in a large, deep-sided roasting pan over moderate heat. Lightly brown both cut sides of each wedge of pumpkin, turning them over as each one colors using kitchen tongs.

Set the oven at 425°F/200°C. Lay the wedges of pumpkin on their side in a roasting pan, then pour in the hot chicken or vegetable stock and seal the roasting pan with aluminum foil. Bake for forty-five minutes, then remove the foil, turn the pieces of pumpkin over, and baste them thoroughly with the stock. Return to the oven and continue cooking for another forty-five minutes. The pumpkin should be translucent, each slice heavy with stock.

Carefully lift the pumpkin from the stock and set aside on a warm serving dish. Place the stock over a fierce heat and let it reduce to about ¾ cup plus two tablespoons/200ml. Pour in the cream, then stir in the two mustards, a little at a time, until you have a warmth you like. Season with salt and black pepper.

Spoon the mustard sauce on the slices of pumpkin and serve.

(continued)

• You can cook any of the golden-fleshed autumn squashes in the style of fondant potatoes. That is, lightly browned in a little oil or butter, then baked in stock until they become saturated with the liquor, almost glowing. A texture so soft and giving as to be almost like sorbet. Such a recipe takes patience but little hands-on work.

• You need to baste the squash with stock once or perhaps twice during its sojourn in the oven. Cooked in this way, pieces of pumpkin make a juicy side dish, but I enjoy them as a course in their own right, with the sauce above, where the cooking juices are bolstered with cream and mustard.

SWEET POTATO, JALAPEÑO, BEANS

Sweet heat.

Serves 2

a large sweet potato
radishes 4
a jalapeño

butter ¼ cup/50g
black-eyed peas 1 × 15-oz/400g can
mozzarella 3½ oz/100g

Set the oven at 425°F/200°C, pierce the skin of the sweet potato with a fork a few times, and bake it for forty-five minutes to an hour till the inside is soft and melting.

Slice the potato in half and scoop out the filling with a spoon, keeping the skin as intact as possible (it will be a little fragile), and mash with a fork. Cut the radishes into matchsticks. Thinly slice the jalapeño.

Warm the butter in a large frying pan, add the jalapeño and fry for two minutes, then tip in the drained beans. Stir in the mashed sweet potato, season with salt, and cook for three or four minutes. Tear the mozzarella into pieces and add to the sweet potato, then spoon back into the potato skins.

Scatter the matchstick radishes over the top and serve.

• You can use a floury potato like russet instead should you wish, but the sweet potato seems to sit particularly happily with the beans and the coolness of the mozzarella.

• Use whatever beans you have on hand. Navy, cannellini, and lima beans will all fit the bill.

• The radishes add a pleasing crunch to each mouthful of soft potato and cheese. Use daikon if you prefer, or cool, crisp cucumber.

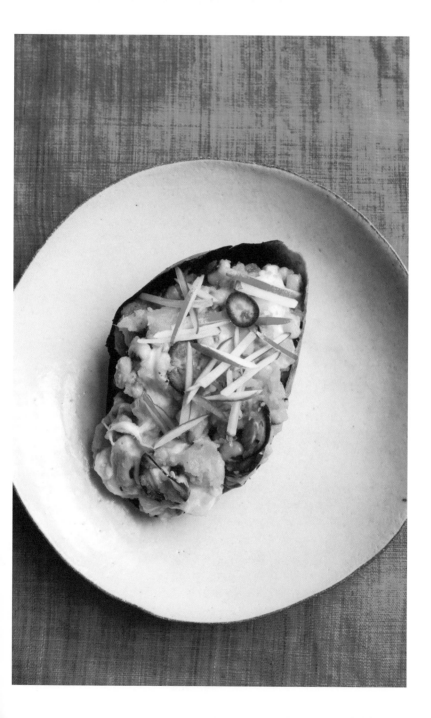

SWEET POTATOES, TOMATOES

Soft, spiced mash. Sharp, sweet, roasted tomatoes.

Serves 3-4

sweet potatoes 1 lb 14 oz/850g
cherry tomatoes on the vine
   1 lb 2 oz/500g
olive oil 8 tablespoons/120ml
onions, medium 2

garlic 2 medium cloves
ground turmeric 2 teaspoons
yellow mustard seeds
   3 teaspoons

Set the oven at 425°F/200°C. Peel the sweet potatoes and cut them in half lengthwise, then into thick chunks, as you might for boiling. Place in a steamer basket over a pot of boiling water, then cover with a tight lid and let them steam to tenderness — a matter of twenty minutes or so. Test them every five minutes with a skewer.

Put the tomatoes in a shallow baking dish, tossing them with half the olive oil and seasoning with just a little salt. Roast for about twenty minutes until their skins have blackened. While the sweet potatoes steam and the tomatoes roast, peel and thinly slice the onions, and cook them in the remaining olive oil in a shallow pan until they are soft and golden. Peel and thinly slice the garlic and stir it into the softening onions. When the onions and garlic are soft and golden, scoop them out into a small bowl.

Drain the juices from the tomatoes into the pan used for the onions and place over moderate heat. Stir in the turmeric, letting it sizzle for a moment, then add the mustard seeds and a little black pepper. As soon as the mustard seeds start to pop, remove from the heat. Mash the sweet potatoes with a potato masher, then stir in the turmeric, mustard seeds, and cooking juices.

Spoon the spiced sweet potato mash onto plates, then add the cooked onions and garlic, and the roasted tomatoes. *(continued)*

• As the tomatoes roast, their juices will leak into the olive oil, forming a sweet-sharp base for the mustard seeds and turmeric. A handful of curry leaves, tossed in with the mustard seeds, wouldn't go amiss. Let the leaves warm for a minute or two in the hot oil with the mustard seeds, just long enough to lightly infuse the dressing with their earthy warmth.

ON A PLATE

My father's generation wouldn't have countenanced salad on a winter's day. But our eating moves on. Winter leaves, particularly the chicories, come into their own in cold weather; apples and pears are at their juiciest on a crisp autumn day; nuts and mushrooms are some of the finest ingredients the season has to offer.

On a golden autumn afternoon, I will make a salad of soft, freckled leaves of lettuce, with blackberries and blue cheese, and toss them in a dressing of cider vinegar and walnuts. As the nights draw in, mushrooms will be marinated with orange juice and sherry vinegar, then sprinkled with toasted hazelnuts and toasted white breadcrumbs. In deep midwinter, beets will be baked and eaten warm with white-tipped radishes, mint, and segments of blood orange.

I will not forgo my love of leaves, tufts of watercress, and ice-crisp raw vegetables just because there's a fire in the hearth. A plate of salad leaves is not just for summer. While they are unlikely to form the main course, arrangements of raw vegetables sit comfortably aside a bowl of deep ochre soup and a lump of open-textured bread torn from a sourdough loaf.

The trick is in the dressing. Walnut and sesame oils, pickling liquors and cider vinegars, toasted nuts, and grain and smooth mustards all marry with the ingredients of the season — the russet-skinned apples, fat juicy pears, hot mustardy leaves, and crunchy white celery.

The fragile salad leaves of summer give way to shreds of red and white cabbage, onions fast-pickled in white wine vinegar, tight bulbs of chicory, thin slices of fennel (marinate them in lemon juice to soften their aniseed notes), and finely sliced raw kale. There is a robustness to a composition of winter vegetables that is very different from the immature and tender leaves of summer. Stems are thicker and more crunchy, leaves have more bite, flavors are more assertive.

Serving food on a plate does give the ingredients a chance to shine, but I think we should avoid the temptation to tinker just to make something look attractive. By all means hand over a tempting-looking plate of food, but nothing good will come from plated arrangements. Letting food fall naturally into place will always look more appetizing than food that has been "arranged."

APPLES, BLUE CHEESE, WALNUTS

Crisp apples and toasted nuts. The colors of autumn.

Serves 2
For the dressing:
blackberries ½ cup/65g
cider vinegar ¼ cup/60ml
walnut oil 3 tablespoons
olive oil 3 tablespoons

walnut halves ⅔ cup/75g
a large apple
blackberries ½ cup/60g
a winter lettuce such as
    Castelfranco
blue cheese such as Shropshire
    Blue, Stilton, or Stichelton
    9 oz/250g

Make the dressing: put the blackberries, cider vinegar, and the oils into a food processor and blend for a few seconds, then tip into a salad bowl.

Toast the walnut halves in a dry pan till warm and fragrant, then add to the dressing. Quarter, core, and slice the apple and gently toss with the walnuts, blackberries, and dressing. Tear the lettuce into large pieces, teasing the heart leaves apart, then divide between two plates. Spoon the dressing on the leaves then crumble the cheese on top.

• Instead of the lettuce, use finely shredded cabbage or sauerkraut. Blueberries can replace the blackberries and pear can be used instead of the apple.

BEET, BLOOD ORANGE, WATERCRESS

Bright flavors for a cold day.

Serves 2

beets, small raw 14 oz/400g
olive oil 1 tablespoon
radishes 8
blood oranges 2
watercress 5 cups/100g
mint leaves 10

parsley leaves a handful
pumpkin seeds 2 tablespoons

For the dressing:
blood orange juice 2 tablespoons
sherry vinegar 2 tablespoons

Set the oven at 425°F/200°C. Place a large piece of aluminum foil in a roasting pan. Wash and trim the beets, taking care not to break their skins, and place them in the foil. Add the olive oil, 2 tablespoons of water, and a grinding of salt and pepper, then scrunch the edges of the foil together to seal. Bake the beets for forty-five to sixty minutes till tender to the point of a knife, then remove and set aside.

Slice the radishes in half and put them in a mixing bowl. Slice the peel from the oranges, taking care to keep any escaping juice, remove the skin from the segments, then add to the radishes. Peel the beets and cut each one in half, then into quarters, and add to the mixing bowl.

Wash and trim the watercress. (I like to dunk it in a bowl of ice water for twenty minutes to crisp up.) Put the mint and parsley leaves into the orange and beet together with the trimmed watercress and pumpkin seeds.

Make the dressing: put the blood orange juice in a small bowl, add the sherry vinegar, season with salt and pepper then pour over the salad and toss gently.

MUSHROOMS, ORANGE, BREADCRUMBS

Bosky flavors. Toasted crumbs.

Serves 4

juice of a blood orange
juice of a lemon
olive oil ¼ cup/60ml
sherry vinegar 2 tablespoons
brown button mushrooms
    9 oz/250g
black figs 8

For the crumbs:
hazelnuts, skinned ½ cup/75g
white bread 1¾ oz/50g
olive oil ¼ cup/60ml
chopped parsley a handful
oakleaf lettuce 1, small
green olives, pitted ¼ cup/35g

Mix together the orange and lemon juices, olive oil, and vinegar, then grind in a little salt and pepper. Thinly slice the mushrooms, put them into the marinade, then cover the bowl and set aside.

Roughly chop the hazelnuts, then toast them in a dry, shallow pan. Set aside in a bowl. Process the bread to coarse crumbs. Warm the olive oil in the same pan over moderate heat, then add the breadcrumbs and toss them gently in the hot oil till pale gold. Stir in the chopped parsley and toasted hazelnuts and set aside.

Tear the lettuce into large pieces and divide among four plates or bowls, then add the marinated mushrooms, the toasted crumbs, and lastly the figs, cut into quarters, and the olives, halved if you like.

• Add other seeds and nuts to the crumbs as you wish. When the crumbs are frying, add pumpkin or sunflower seeds, a sprinkling of chia, a handful of golden raisins, or some sliced almonds.
• Instead of the crumbs, use cooked couscous, quinoa, or puffed rice.

RED CABBAGE, CARROTS, SMOKED ALMONDS

Crisp, crunchy, sour, and smoky. A cabbage salad for a winter's day.

Serves 4

a red onion
malt vinegar 3 tablespoons
cider vinegar 5 tablespoons/75ml
water ½ cup/120ml
yellow mustard seeds 1 teaspoon
red cabbage 1 lb/450g
carrots 9 oz/250g
a pear
smoked almonds a handful
   or two

For the dressing:

sour cream ⅔ cup/150g
pickling liquor from the onion
   ¼ cup/60ml
Dijon mustard 1 teaspoon
grain mustard 1 teaspoon
poppy seeds 1 tablespoon

Peel the onion and finely slice into rings. Warm the vinegars, water, and the mustard seeds in a small saucepan and add half a teaspoon of salt and the onion. Bring to a boil, then remove from the heat, cover, and let pickle for twenty-five minutes.

Finely shred the red cabbage. Peel the carrots, then slice them into long shavings with a vegetable peeler. Halve, core, and slice the pear. Toss the cabbage, carrots, and pear with a little of the onion pickling liquid.

Make the dressing: lightly beat the sour cream, onion pickling liquor, mustards, and poppy seeds. Fold the dressing into the shredded cabbage, carrots, and pear. Finally, add the smoked almonds and the pickled onions, drained of their remaining pickling liquor.

• Should smoked almonds prove elusive, make your own by mixing smoked salt with a little paprika and peanut oil, then toast in a dry pan, before adding the whole almonds.

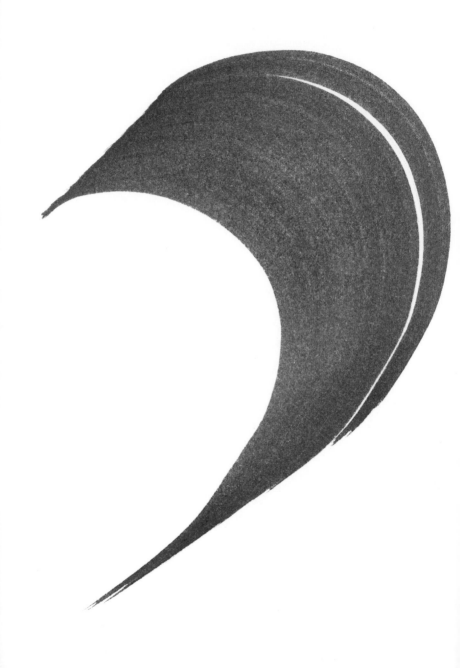

WITH A CRUST

You push your spoon through the crust. The pastry, potato, toasted cheese, or crumbs give under its weight. A puff of aromatic steam. Steam scented with onions and bay, thyme or rosemary, tarragon or garlic. And then your spoon sinks into the depths below. There may be melting cheese or a cloud of sweet potato, there might be mushrooms, sprouts, or silky shallots. Whatever, it will be something to nourish and soothe, warm the heart and calm the soul.

Of course, your crust may be below the filling. A layer of pastry supporting shallots and apple, or a fan of late autumn plums. Maybe some slices of banana glistening with maple syrup. The pastry may be puff or rich buttery shortcrust, it might have chopped thyme rubbed into it, or grated parmesan.

Food cooked with a crust is both soft and crisp. I am not sure food can get better than this on a winter's night. A puff-pastry parcel filled with mashed sweet potato; a deep dish of filo pastry filled with almost-liquid melted Taleggio and toothsome greens. Layers of rutabaga, mushrooms, and Gruyère with a crumbly thyme-freckled wrapper of shortcrust; an herb crumble baked on top of a cream sauce in which sleep tomatoes, leeks, and basil.

I delight in crusts that split here and there. Holes and tears and gaps where the filling peeps deliciously through. Sometimes it floods the pastry: something I always hope for but which happens all too rarely — a tantalizing glimpse of what lies beneath. Be it creamy or simmering in its own juices, spiced or herbed, piping hot or served relaxed and at room temperature, the filling is all the better for having a little of the crust come with it.

I rarely put pastry both under and on top of the filling. The base often fails to crisp at all. And yet a single sheet of pre-rolled puff pastry can be draped over any vegetable stew and baked; a few sheets of filo, each brushed with melted butter (and, if you wish, crumbs or chopped thyme) can provide an instant tart base. For everyday eating I would go for a top or bottom crust, not both.

And although this chapter is complete in itself, it would be remiss of me not to point you in the direction of the dessert chapter, and the quickest banana and maple syrup tarts.

FILO PASTRY, CHEESE, GREENS

A tart to eat straight from the oven, while the cheese is still soft and melting.

Serves 4

purple sprouting broccoli or
  broccolini 9 oz/250g
sprout tops 5¼ oz/150g
butter 6 tablespoons/90g

filo pastry sheets, defrosted
  9½ oz/270g (about ½ of a
  1-lb/455g package)
Taleggio 1 lb 2 oz/500g
parmesan 5¼ oz/150g

Bring a large, deep pot of water to a boil. Set the oven at 425°F/200°C. Place a baking sheet or pizza stone in the oven. Slice each stem of purple sprouting broccoli in half lengthwise. Finely shred the sprout tops. Lower the broccoli into the boiling water, cook for three or four minutes till the color is bright, then lift out with a slotted spoon and refresh in a bowl of ice water. Do the same with the shredded sprout tops.

Melt the butter in a small pan. Brush the base of a 12-inch round baking dish or tart pan with some of the butter, lay a sheet of pastry over the base and brush it with more butter. Repeat with the remaining sheets of pastry, letting them overhang the edges of the pan.

Tear the Taleggio into small pieces and grate the parmesan. Drain the vegetables and dry on paper towels. Fill the tart case with the drained purple sprouting broccoli and sprout tops, then tuck the Taleggio among them and scatter the grated parmesan. Fold the overhanging pastry back over the edges of the tart, place on the heated stone or baking sheet, and bake for twenty to twenty-five minutes, till the pastry is crisp.

• Putting a metal baking sheet or pizza stone in the oven before you start is a sound idea. As the oven warms, the sheet will heat up, providing an extra-hot base on which to bake your tart. Doing this will ensure a crisper base than if you simply place the tart on the oven shelf.

LEEKS, PARSNIPS, PASTRY

Bosky vegetables. Cream sauce. Crisp crust.

Serves 4

leeks, medium 2
butter 3 tablespoons
brown button mushrooms
    7 oz/200g
olive oil ¼ cup/60ml
parsnips 14 oz/400g

smoked garlic 4 cloves
thyme 12 sprigs
heavy cream 1½ cups/350ml
defrosted puff pastry
    1 (11½ oz/245g) sheet
a small egg, beaten

Set the oven at 425°F/200°C. Cut the leeks into ¾-inch/2cm-thick rings and wash them thoroughly. Put the leeks in a saucepan with the butter, place a piece of parchment paper over the surface of the leeks, then cover tightly with a lid. Let the leeks steam in the butter over moderate heat until tender, but not colored.

Thickly slice the mushrooms. In a shallow ovenproof pan about 10 inches/25cm in diameter, warm the olive oil, add the mushrooms, and fry till golden. Meanwhile, peel the parsnips and cut into ½-inch/1cm dice. Peel and thinly slice the garlic. Remove the mushrooms as they are ready, then add the parsnips to the pan, together with a little more oil if necessary. Let them brown lightly, adding the garlic after five minutes, then remove them and return the mushrooms to the pan.

When the leeks are tender, remove the lid and paper and add the leeks and parsnips to the mushrooms. Season the cream with salt, pepper, and the sprigs of thyme, then pour over the vegetables, remove from the heat, and let cool a little.

Roll the pastry out into a disk large enough to cover the pie. Lower the pastry into place over the vegetables, pressing it tightly over the edges. Brush with the beaten egg, then cut a small hole in the center to let the steam out. Bake for twenty-five minutes till pale gold and the cream is bubbling.

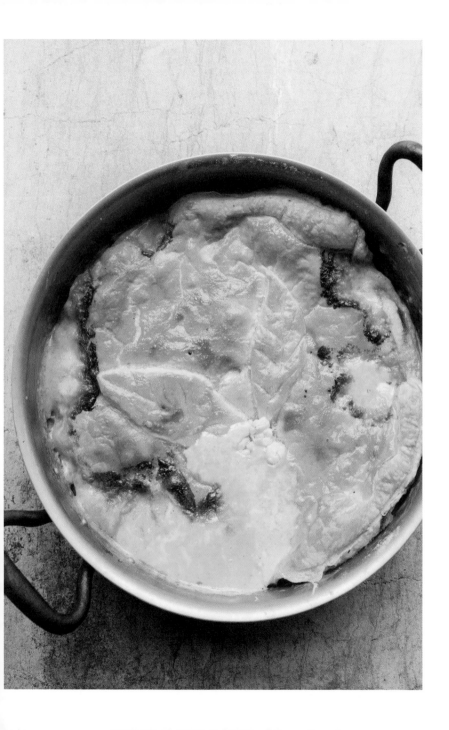

LEEKS, TOMATO, PECORINO

Hearty but not heavy.

Serves 4
leeks 1 lb 14 oz/850g
butter 3 tablespoons
cherry tomatoes 10½ oz/300g
basil leaves ½ cup/10g
heavy cream 1 cup/240ml

For the crumble:
all-purpose flour 2 cups/250g
chilled butter ½ cup plus
  1 tablespoon/125g
Pecorino, grated 2½ oz/75g
thyme sprigs ⅓ oz/10g
parsley ¾ cup/15g

Cut the white and light green parts of the leeks into ½-inch/1cm-thick rounds, then wash very thoroughly in cold water. Put the leeks into a deep ovenproof casserole or saucepan with the butter, cover with a lid, and let them soften over moderate heat. A regular stir will stop them from coloring. Cut the tomatoes in half and stir into the softening leeks, together with some sea salt and black pepper, letting them cook for about ten minutes until soft and juicy. Stir in the basil leaves, then the cream. When the cream has warmed, remove from the heat. Set the oven at 425°F/200°C.

Make the crumble: put the flour in a large mixing bowl, add the butter in small pieces, and rub in with your fingertips. Stir in the grated cheese. Pull the leaves from the thyme and parsley, finely chop, and stir in to the crumble. You can do this in seconds in a food processor. Sprinkle several drops of water over the mixture and shake the bowl back and forth until you have a mixture of large and small crumbs. Scatter the crumble over the tomato and leeks then bake for forty minutes till bubbling round the edges.

• Parmesan or a firm, extra-mature cheddar, grated finely, will do the job of the Pecorino if you prefer. Rosemary, finely chopped, can work in place of thyme, or you could use herbes de Provence.

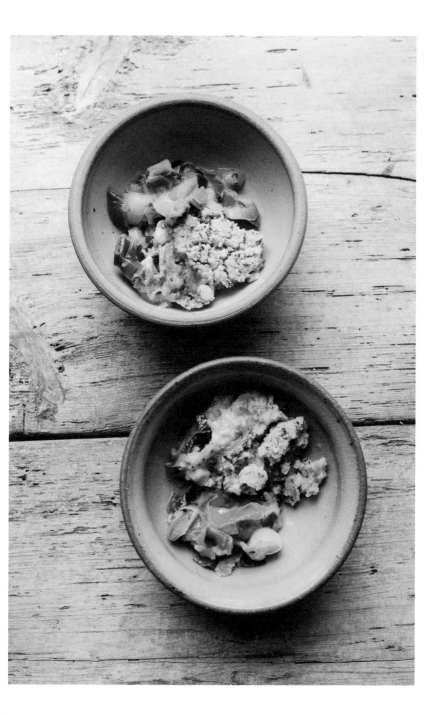

SHALLOTS, APPLES, PARMESAN

A classic tart. A savory twist.

Serves 6

For the pastry:

all-purpose flour 1¾ cups/225g

chilled butter ½ cup plus 2 tablespoons/150g

egg yolk 1

thyme leaves 2 teaspoons

parmesan, finely grated 4 tablespoons/30g

shallots, medium 4

olive oil 2 tablespoons

apples 2

You will need a tarte Tatin pan or an ovenproof frying pan measuring 10 inches/25cm in diameter.

Put the flour into the bowl of a food processor, add ½ cup/120g butter in small pieces, and process to the texture of fine breadcrumbs. Add the egg, thyme, and 3 tablespoons of the parmesan and process briefly. Add a few tablespoons of cold water to produce a soft, rollable dough. Transfer to a lightly floured board and bring together into a ball. Wrap in parchment paper or place in a bowl and cover, and let rest in the fridge.

Set the oven at 425°F/200°C. Peel the shallots, then halve lengthwise. Melt the remaining two tablespoons of butter with the oil in the pan or frying pan over moderate heat, then add the shallots, cut side down. Let them brown lightly, then turn to let the other side color. Meanwhile, halve, core, and slice each apple into eight segments. Remove the shallots from the pan, then add the apples, letting them soften and turn lightly gold. Scatter the remaining 1 tablespoon of grated parmesan, then return the shallots.

Roll the pastry out to a good 1¼ inches/3cm larger than the pan or frying pan. Lay the pastry over the shallots and apples, tucking in the overhanging dough. Bake for twenty-five minutes, until the pastry is pale cookie-colored and the butter is bubbling round the edges. Remove from the oven, let settle for ten minutes, then turn out onto a serving plate.

RUTABAGA, MUSHROOM, GRUYÈRE, THYME

Herb scented, rib-sticking filling. Crumbly pastry.

Serves 6
For the pastry:
all-purpose flour 1⅔ cups/200g
rye or whole wheat flour ¾ cup
    plus 2 tablespoons/100g
thyme leaves 1 tablespoon
chilled butter ½ cup plus
    2 tablespoons/150g
salt a pinch

an egg, beaten

For the filling:
a medium onion
butter 6 tablespoons/90g
rutabaga 1 lb/450g
brown button mushrooms
    9 oz/250g
Gruyère 9 oz/250g

Make the pastry: put both the flours and the thyme leaves in a large bowl, cut the butter into small pieces, then add it with the salt to the flour and rub together with your fingertips until you have a breadcrumb-like consistency. Introduce enough cold water to produce a soft, rollable dough. Alternatively, you could make this in a food processor. Turn out onto a floured work surface, pat into a ball, flatten the top, then wrap in parchment paper and refrigerate for thirty minutes.

Set the oven at 425°F/200°C. Place an upturned baking sheet or pizza stone in the oven to heat up. Peel and roughly chop the onion then let it soften in 2 tablespoons of the butter over medium heat in a large, wide pan. Peel the rutabaga, cut each in half lengthwise, then cut each half into quarters. Slice each quarter thinly. Remove the onion from the pan — it should be pale gold and translucent. Add the pieces of rutabaga to the pan, adding more butter if necessary, turning them as they brighten and soften. Thinly slice the mushrooms, then add them to the pan, with the remaining butter, and cook till pale gold. Grate the Gruyère into a large bowl, then add the rutabaga, onions, and mushrooms. Season generously with black pepper. *(continued)*

On the floured board, roll the pastry out into a large, rough-edged circle approximately 12 inches/30cm in diameter and transfer to a parchment-lined or flour-dusted baking sheet. Pile the filling in the center of the pastry, leaving a wide gap of bare pastry round the edge. Fold the edges of the pastry over the filling, leaving the middle open. Brush the edges with beaten egg, then place the whole baking sheet on top of the hot sheet or stone in the oven and cook for twenty-five minutes, till the pastry is pale gold and the filling has crisped on top. Let settle for ten minutes before slicing.

• This is rather good cold too, and can be sliced and tucked inside a lunchbox or taken on a picnic.

SWEET POTATO, PUFF PASTRY

Crisp pastry. Soft, mildly spicy stuffing.

Serves 4

sweet potatoes 1 lb 14 oz/850g
harissa paste 2 teaspoons
ras el hanout 1 teaspoon
defrosted puff pastry
   2 (8½ oz/245g) sheets

an egg
black sesame seeds a couple
   of pinches

Set the oven at 425°F/200°C. Place an empty baking sheet in the oven to warm. (It will help the base of your pastry to crisp.) Put a pot of water on to boil and balance a steamer basket or colander over it. Peel the sweet potatoes, cut them into large pieces, and steam for ten to fifteen minutes until tender. Remove from the steamer, then mash with a potato masher or fork till smooth. Season with sea salt, the harissa paste, and the ras el hanout, and set aside to cool.

Working with one sheet of pastry at a time, roll the pastry out to a rectangle measuring 14 × 9 inches/35 × 23cm, then transfer to a baking sheet lined with parchment paper, turning the pastry so the long side is facing you. Spoon half of the cooled sweet potato on the right-hand half, leaving a ¼-inch/2cm rim around the edge uncovered, then smooth the surface flat.

Break the egg into a small bowl and beat lightly with a fork to mix yolk and white. Brush the bare edge generously with the beaten egg, then fold the left-hand side over the right, as if you were closing a book, and press firmly around the edges to seal.

Score a trellis pattern on the top of each pastry, then brush with more of the beaten egg. Scatter the black sesame seeds over the top, then bake for thirty to thirty-five minutes on the hot baking sheet till golden brown.

(continued)

• The filling should be soft but not wet. Should you choose to boil the sweet potato instead of steaming, make sure to drain thoroughly, and let cool uncovered for ten minutes to allow the steam to escape.

• I have also made this with floury-fleshed potatoes such as russet, adding a handful of grated cheese after mashing. A deeply satisfying pie for a cold day.

WITH A LADLE

A ladle is the spirit of generosity. Deeply comforting, capacious, motherly. A ladle is a spoon that is expecting friends for dinner. (Even the largest kitchen spoon feels inadequate beside the smallest ladle.) Generosity that goes beyond mere quantity. You dip your ladle deep into a pot of soup or stew and lift out enough to fill the hungriest of diners, a bowl of steaming savor and sustenance. Full to the brim, overflowing with welcome.

And yet what we serve from a ladle is often humble — a soup of beans and woody herbs; a piping-hot onion broth; a scented stew of noodles and spices. No matter how basic the ingredients, the food we share from this piece of bent metal is at once hearty and wholesome.

A ladle doesn't do dainty, twee, or tight-fisted. It doesn't do lonely. You don't often serve your own dinner with a ladle. Like a pot of tea, this is a piece of equipment that is about sharing something with others. You may ask everyone to help themselves to a spoonful of pie. To cut themselves a slice of bread. But it is invariably the cook who wields the ladle.

Some foods ask to be served from this bowl-on-a-handle. Broth obviously, smooth vegetable purées too, but also lumpy soups and wannabe stews. But nothing with a crust, which needs a wide spoon to ensure the pastry or crumb topping stays on top. A ladle is there for a soup of black-eyed peas and greens; small seed-shaped pasta with grated cheese and herbs; a creamy purée made from a cauliflower or pumpkin and, of course, stock.

My first ladle, taken from a restaurant that had more than it needed, was too wide. The soup gushed over the sides of the narrow-mouthed bowls I had at the time. The second, a gift from a friend (which surely belonged with a silver-plate tureen in a grand restaurant), had a flamboyant kink in the handle that made it uncomfortable to hold. It twisted as you poured. The next had a handle too upright from the bowl and made aiming the contents difficult. It left a few stains behind.

The handle should sit at a slight angle to the bowl, so it pours comfortably as you turn your hand to the left (assuming you are right-handed), which rules out most of those sold in catering supply shops, whose handles seem to sit straight against the bowl. And they must have a hook or a sharp bend at the end, so you can hang them by the cooker, which is where they are going to be of most use. I don't think it should be stainless steel, too clinical and coldhearted. The one I have settled with is made of white enamel, a little chipped now, and has been with me for so long it feels like an old friend.

The right ladle, like the right knife, is the one that feels made for your hand. Ideally, it should look as much at home at the table as it does in the kitchen. A cheap one will probably work as well as any. Try before you buy. Hold it aloft in the shop and scoop bowlfuls of air into an imaginary soup bowl. How does it feel? A good ladle is a friend for life, and will be a friend to your friends, who are sitting patiently at the table, waiting for you to turn up with it in your hand.

BEET, LENTILS, GARAM MASALA

Soft, soothing spice.

Serves 4

a medium onion
olive oil 3 tablespoons
garlic 2 cloves
chile flakes 2 teaspoons
yellow mustard seeds 1 teaspoon
vegetable stock 3⅓ cups/800ml
split orange lentils
    1½ cups/300g

cooked beet 9 oz/250g
butter ¼ cup/50g
garam masala 4 teaspoons
plain whole milk yogurt
    ¼ cup/65g

Peel the onion and slice into rings. Pour the oil into a shallow pan, add the onions, then fry to a deep, golden brown — a good twenty-five minutes — stirring from time to time. Peel and thinly slice the garlic, adding it to the onions halfway through cooking. Stir in the chile flakes and mustard seeds and continue cooking for a couple of minutes.

Bring the stock to a boil in a medium saucepan, tip in the lentils, lower the heat slightly, then let them cook for fifteen minutes till soft.

Roughly chop the beet and fold into the lentils, adding the butter and garam masala, then check the seasoning, adding salt and black pepper as necessary. Continue cooking for three or four minutes, then spoon into bowls.

Spoon the onions and yogurt on top, stirring each bowl thoroughly to mix the onions, mustard, and chile into the dal as you eat.

• Mild and slightly sweet, this lentil dish becomes interesting when you stir in the yogurt and spiced onions. Increase the chile level to suit your taste, or introduce a little mashed fresh ginger.

BEET, SAUERKRAUT, DILL

The sweetness of beets. The sourness of cabbage. The heat of horseradish.

Serves 2

vegetable stock 2½ cups/600ml
cooked beet 1 lb 2 oz/500g
sauerkraut ⅔ cup/100g
dill, chopped ¼ cup/5g

sour cream ⅔ cup/160g
fresh horseradish a thumb-sized piece

Bring the stock to a boil in a large saucepan. Put the beet in the bowl of a food processor and process to a coarse purée. Stir the beet into the stock and season generously with black pepper and a little salt.

Mix the sauerkraut with the dill. Ladle the beet and stock into deep bowls. Divide the sauerkraut between them, then spoon on the sour cream. Finely grate about a teaspoon of horseradish (to taste) over the surface of the soup.

• I use whichever stock is on hand for soups such as this. Homemade if I have it, otherwise bought pre-made or made up from bouillon powder. They all have their merits.
• Sauerkraut is one of those ever-present ingredients in my fridge, like yogurt, lemons, and tsukemono, the jewel-hued Japanese pickles. I buy it in jars or packets and dip into it on an almost daily basis. It makes a refreshing accompaniment to almost anything you care to mention.

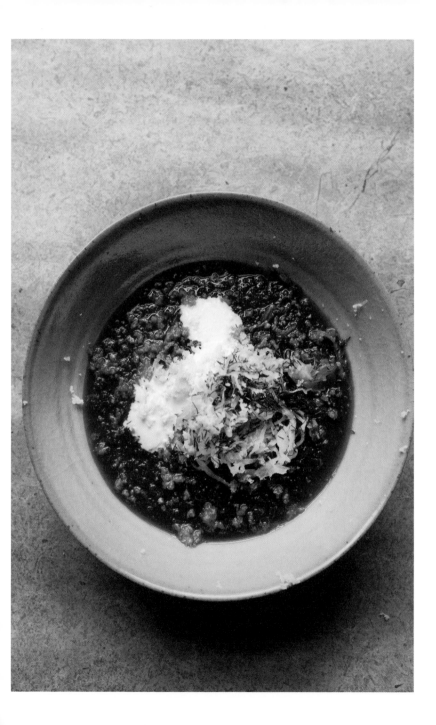

BEANS, ROSEMARY, KALE

Therapy for a cold, wet winter's night.

Serves 4

a large onion
a large, fat carrot
rosemary 2 sprigs
celery 2 sticks
garlic 2 cloves
olive oil 3 tablespoons
a large tomato
black-eyed peas
    2 × 15-oz/400g cans

vegetable stock 3¼ cups/750ml
bay leaves 2

To finish:
kale or Brussels sprout tops 150g
parsley leaves a good handful
olive oil

Peel and roughly chop the onion and the carrot. Pull the needles from the rosemary and chop finely. Remove the leaves from the celery and reserve, then chop the stalks into small pieces. Peel and finely chop the garlic.

Warm the olive oil in a wide, deep saucepan. When the oil is hot, add the onion, carrot, rosemary, celery, and garlic and cook over low to moderate heat for about fifteen minutes, till the vegetables are starting to soften. Roughly chop and stir in the tomato.

Tip the beans in with the vegetables, rinsing them first if you wish, then pour in the vegetable stock (or water) and bring to a boil. Add the bay leaves, lower the heat, then simmer for fifteen minutes until hot. Season generously with salt and black pepper. Ladle one-third of the mixture into a blender, process till smooth, then stir back into the soup.

Pick over the kale or sprout tops and tear into small pieces. Dunk the kale or sprout leaves under the surface of the soup and leave to soften for two or three minutes. Roughly chop the parsley and the reserved celery leaves. Ladle the soup into bowls, scatter the surface with the chopped celery and parsley leaves, and finish with a trickle of olive oil.

BRUSSELS TOPS, BLUE CHEESE

The goodness of greens. The savor of cheese.

Serves 4

milk 2½ cups/600ml
Stilton 7 oz/200g
onions 2
butter 2 tablespoons
Brussels sprout tops 12¼ oz/350g

To finish:
the reserved sprouts (from
    the tops)
butter 2 tablespoons
Stilton 3½ oz/100g, crumbled

Bring the milk to a boil, then remove from the heat. Crumble the Stilton into the milk, cover with a lid, and let infuse. Peel the onions, then roughly chop them.

Melt the butter in a large, deep pan and add the chopped onion. Fry gently over moderate heat for about ten minutes, until the onion is glossy and sweet smelling, stirring regularly. Pull the sprout leaves from the main stem, setting aside any whole tiny sprouts you may find. Remove the stems from the leaves and chop them, then stir into the onions.

Place the leaves on top of one another, roll them up, then slice into thin shreds and stir into the onion. Continue cooking for five minutes until the leaves are bright green and wilted. Pour in the milk and cheese mixture and bring almost to a boil. Ladle into a blender, taking care not to overfill (you will need to do this in two batches) and process to a thick but far from totally smooth soup. Check the flavor, adding black pepper if necessary. The soup is unlikely to need salt.

To finish, cut the reserved sprouts in half and fry them for a minute or so in the butter until they are bright and crunchy. Toss them with the crumbled Stilton and divide among the bowls.

CELERY ROOT, HORSERADISH, PUMPERNICKEL

A soup to soothe the soul.

Serves 4

celery root 2 lb 2 oz/1kg
vegetable stock 1⅔ cups/400ml
milk 2½ cups/600ml
chives scant 1 oz/25g
olive oil ½ cup/120ml

grated horseradish root
  1 tablespoon
pumpernickel or other rye
  bread 3½ oz/100g

Peel and roughly chop the celery root, then place in a deep pan with the stock and milk and bring to a boil. Lower the heat and simmer for twenty minutes.

While the soup is simmering, chop the chives and put them in a blender with the olive oil. Blitz to a bright green dressing.

Purée the celery root mixture, in two or three batches, using a blender. If you have an immersion blender, then process it directly in the pan. Stir the horseradish into the soup and check the seasoning. Crumble the pumpernickel and toast briefly till lightly crisp in a dry, shallow pan.

Ladle the soup into bowls, pour in the chive oil, and scatter the pumpernickel.

• Celery root is one of the more undersung vegetables, but has plenty going for it. I like it shredded and stirred into a mustardy mayonnaise, but also coarsely grated and fried in olive oil and butter until golden and sizzling and served with a spritz of lemon.

CHEDDAR, CIDER, MUSTARD

Deep bowls of velvety soup.

Serves 6

onions, medium 2
butter 2 tablespoons
olive oil a little
carrots, medium 2
celery 1 stick
milk 1⅔ cups/400ml
all-purpose flour
    6 tablespoons/45g

vegetable stock 1⅔ cups/400ml
cider 1½ cups/350ml
grain mustard 1 teaspoon
cheddar 14 oz/400g
chopped parsley a small handful
crusty bread, for serving

Peel and roughly chop the onions. Warm the butter and oil in a deep saucepan over moderate heat, then add the onions and cook till soft. Scrub and finely dice the carrots, finely dice the celery, then add to the softening onion and continue cooking for ten minutes or so till tender.

Warm the milk in a small saucepan and set aside. Stir the flour into the vegetables and continue cooking for two or three minutes, then add the milk and stir to a thick sauce. Pour in the vegetable stock and cider, bring it to a boil, then lower the heat and let the mixture simmer for a few minutes. Stir in the mustard and check the seasoning. (It may want pepper, but probably very little salt.)

Grate the cheese and stir into the soup, leaving it to simmer (it is crucial it doesn't boil) for five minutes, until the soup has thickened. Add a handful of parsley as you bring it to the table, and serve with bread.

• Use a mature, full-flavored cheddar here. The stock should, if possible, be homemade, chicken or vegetable. Bread is a nonnegotiable either torn and placed in the base of the soup bowl, the soup ladled over it, or toasted and dipped into the soup's creamy depths in fat, jagged chunks.

FENNEL, CUCUMBER, MINT

A chilled soup for a warm autumn day.

Serves 4

fennel 14 oz/400g
butter 5 tablespoons/75g
water ½ cup/120ml
juice of half a lemon
cucumber 10½ oz/300g
radishes 12

pickle juice (from a jar of
cornichons) or white wine
vinegar 2 tablespoons
mint leaves 12
yogurt 1 cup/250g
ice cubes

Thinly slice the fennel. Melt the butter in a deep pan, add the water, lemon juice, and fennel, and cover with a piece of parchment paper. Cover with a lid and cook for about twenty minutes over low to moderate heat, so the fennel steams rather than fries, cooking without color. When fully tender, process to a purée in a blender.

Cut the cucumber in half lengthwise, scrape out the seeds with a teaspoon, then grate the flesh coarsely. Grate the radishes and mix with the cucumber. Stir in the pickle juice or vinegar, and the fennel purée, then shred the mint leaves and stir them in, together with the yogurt.

Ladle into bowls, then add a couple of ice cubes to each and, if you wish, a couple of radishes.

• A cool, bright-tasting soup given piquancy with a little juice from the pickle jar. I have also made this slightly thicker, using a strained yogurt, and eaten it with dark rye bread.
• Don't be tempted to serve this soup hot — it curdles when heated. It is my belief that chilled soups must be thoroughly cold. With that in mind I store the soup in the fridge, then serve it with ice cubes dropped in. A brilliant answer as to what to eat for a bright, sunny autumn lunch.

MUSHROOMS, BUTTERNUT, SOUR CREAM

A bowlful of autumn.

Serves 4
butternut squash 2 lb 2 oz/1kg
shallots, medium 6
olive oil 5 tablespoons/75ml
sweet paprika 1 teaspoon
hot smoked paprika 1 teaspoon
vegetable stock 1 quart/1 liter
sour cream ⅔ cup/160g

For the mushrooms:
brown button mushrooms
  7 oz/200g
olive oil 3 tablespoons
ginger 1⅓-oz/10g piece

Set the oven at 425°F/200°C. Peel the butternut, halve it lengthwise, and discard the seeds and fibers. Cut the flesh into large chunks, then place in a single layer on a baking sheet or roasting pan. Peel the shallots, halve them, then tuck them among the squash.

Mix the olive oil and the paprikas, then spoon over the squash, slide the dish into the oven, and bake for about an hour, or until the squash is patchily browned but thoroughly soft and tender.

Warm the vegetable stock in a large saucepan. Add the squash and shallots to the stock, place over moderate heat (use a few spoonfuls of the stock to deglaze the roasting pan if there are any interesting bits of roasted squash and shallot left), then season with salt and a little pepper and bring to a boil. Partially cover the pan with a lid and simmer for twenty minutes, until the squash is falling to pieces. Crush a few pieces of the squash into the liquid with a fork to thicken it slightly.

Slice the mushrooms thinly, then fry them in the olive oil in a shallow pan until golden. Peel the ginger and shred it into very fine matchsticks, then add it to the mushrooms and continue cooking for a minute or two. When all is golden and sizzling, remove from the heat.

Ladle the soup into deep bowls, then spoon in the sour cream and the mushrooms and ginger.

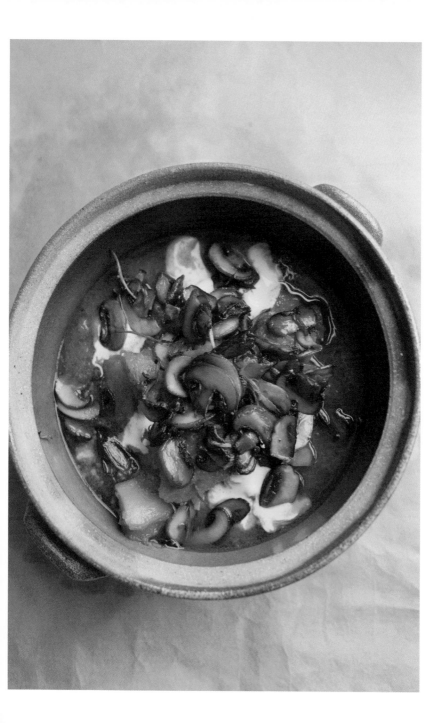

NOODLES, LENTILS, SOUR CREAM

A frugal, rich, and sustaining soup-stew. My version of the Iranian *ash reshteh*.

Serves 4–6

onions 4
olive oil 3 tablespoons
garlic 3 cloves
ground turmeric 2 teaspoons
chickpeas 1 × 15-oz/400g can
navy beans 1 × 15-oz/400g can
small brown lentils ½ cup/100g
vegetable stock 1 quart/1 liter

butter 3 tablespoons
linguine or Iranian reshteh
   noodles 3½ oz/100g
spinach 7 oz/200g
parsley 1½ cups/30g
cilantro 1 cup/20g
mint ¾ cup/15g
sour cream 1 cup/250g

Peel the onions. Roughly chop two of them and thinly slice the others. Warm the olive oil in a large pan set over moderate heat, add the two chopped onions, and fry them for ten to fifteen minutes till soft and pale gold. Peel and thinly slice the garlic, then stir in with the ground turmeric and continue cooking for a couple of minutes.

Drain the chickpeas and beans and stir into the onions together with the lentils and stock. Bring to a boil, then lower the heat and let simmer for thirty minutes, stirring occasionally.

Melt the butter in a shallow pan, then add the reserved sliced onions and let them cook slowly, with the occasional stir, until they are a rich toffee brown. This will take a good half an hour, maybe longer.

Add the noodles to the simmering beans. Wash the spinach, put it in a pan set over medium heat, cover with a lid, and cook for three or four minutes until it has wilted. Turn occasionally with kitchen tongs. Remove the spinach and put it in a colander under cold running water until cool. Wring the moisture from the spinach with your hands, then stir into the simmering stew. Roughly chop the parsley, cilantro, and mint leaves and stir most of them into the onions and beans.   *(continued)*

Fold in the sour cream, then ladle into bowls and fold in the remaining herbs and the fried onions.

• One of the dishes we ate time and again when in Iran, this is a bowl of deep, wholesome goodness. The soup is soothing and sustaining and was much appreciated by our film crew after a long, dusty day's work.
• Traditionally you would use the flat *reshteh* noodles, but any will work, even small round pasta if you prefer. Gently stir all the ingredients together at the table to produce a silky-textured soup-stew.

ORZO, SMOKED MOZZARELLA, THYME

Pale, soft, and deeply comforting. Notes of thyme, cheese, and smoke.

Serves 2

garlic 3 cloves
butter 2 tablespoons
orzo 1 cup/200g
vegetable stock 2 cups/480ml

milk ¾ cup plus 2 tablespoons/ 200ml
thyme 8 bushy sprigs
smoked mozzarella 2¼ oz/60g

Peel and thinly slice the garlic. Warm the butter in a deep pan, add the garlic, and fry for a couple of minutes till pale gold, then add the orzo, stock, and milk and bring to a boil. Pull the leaves from the thyme and add to the pasta together with a half teaspoon of salt, then simmer for fifteen minutes till the orzo is plump, soft, and creamy. The sauce should be similar in texture to a risotto.

Grate the smoked mozzarella, then fold into the orzo with a generous grinding of black pepper.

• If I could choose just one bowl of food for a cold night, it would most likely be this. Understated, calm, and effortlessly easy, it has a comforting texture and the deep, savory satisfaction you get with cheese and pasta.
• There are options here. Change the cheese to a fruity, deeply mature cheddar. Use trofie or strozzapreti pasta in place of the orzo and use smoked garlic for an extra layer of warmth.
• Once the dish is ready, you could also spoon it into a heatproof dish, cover the surface with more grated cheese and broil till bubbling.

TAHINI, SESAME, BUTTERNUT

Sweet and nutty.

Serves 4

butternut squash or pumpkin
   2 lb 2 oz/1kg
vegetable stock 1 quart/1 liter
rosemary 3 or 4 sprigs
sesame seeds 3 tablespoons

olive oil 3 tablespoons
roasted chestnuts, canned or
   vacuum-packed 8
tahini 4 tablespoons/70g

Peel and halve the butternut squash, remove the seeds, and cut into large chunks, then put into a large saucepan with the vegetable stock and bring to a boil. Cover with a lid and let simmer for ten minutes until soft enough to crush.

Ladle the squash and its stock into a blender, process in batches until smooth, and return to the pan. Remove the leaves from the rosemary and finely chop. You need enough to fill a tablespoon. Toast the sesame seeds in a dry, shallow pan over moderate heat until golden, then add the olive oil and the rosemary. Crumble the chestnuts into the pan and cook for a minute or so until all is warm and deeply fragrant.

Bring the soup almost to a boil, checking the seasoning as you go, then ladle into soup bowls. Speckle the soup with a tablespoon of tahini in each bowl, then scatter some of the chestnut and sesame seed seasoning over the surface.

• Some people don't peel butternut squash before using it in a soup. Much depends on the thickness of the skin and the age of the squash. If the skin is thin, then it is fine not to peel it. If you are using a pumpkin, remove the skin. It is important to process the soup in batches rather than all at once, when it is likely to overflow. An immersion blender works a treat.

(continued)

• Use mushrooms instead of the chestnuts. I prefer small brown buttons, sliced in halves or quarters and cooked for a minute or two with the sesame oil and rosemary. A few drops of sesame oil, trickled into the soup as you serve, are worth a thought. I like to eat this soup with thick pieces of toasted sourdough bread, spread with cream cheese.

ON THE STOVE

As the evenings cool, out come the carbs. The row of jars on the top shelf, the glass ones with bright orange rubber rings, their contents beige, brown, creamy-white, or yellow. There is freekeh, the roasted green wheat; fine golden polenta and the brown rices. There is white rice to steam for breakfast and pearl barley to toss with tufts of kale and chalk-white cheese. A frosty night is when tiny beads of fregola get their moment in the moonlight, cooked with blue-black lacinato kale and butter.

The stove, its gas jets on low, is where, for the next few months, we will find pots of lentils ready to be tossed with roast vegetables. It is where fat pearls of mograbia will be cooked in bubbling water, drained, and stirred into thick tomato sauces seasoned with cinnamon and cumin. Those gas flames will also fry parsnips for curry and warm spice pastes to fold through bowls of sticky rice.

A deep-sided pan on the stove is where we can simmer milk to replace stock in a silk-textured risotto and warm coconut milk to calm the curry spices for a sauté of roots and spinach. It is where we could boil fregola for tossing with greens and grated Pecorino, and stir thick polenta to calm ourselves after a hectic day.

I like beige food. Suppers of grains and starches that wrap you in the culinary version of cashmere. But there are also bright, fresh tastes in the recipes that follow. White rice steamed with lime and green cardamom; a lemongrass sauce for sweet potatoes; tomatoes simmered with chile and rice vinegar as a sauce for udon noodles. But the real winners are those eaters who need ballast against the cold — a mound of soft yellow polenta with mushrooms and garlic; eggplants simmered in coconut milk; sweet potatoes with fried croquette-like polenta with an accompanying puddle of melting cheese.

Early in the day, as the mist clears, there is porridge to be made and, later, leftover baked suppers that can be reheated the following day on the stove. (A word of advice: let leftovers come up to room temperature before reheating; keep the heat low and the lid on.) I often use the heat of the stove to make a sauce for what is cooking in the oven. A bubble-up of cream, chopped parsley, and grain-freckled mustard for a baked potato; a cheese sauce for a butter-roasted onion or melted crème fraîche, lemon juice, and chopped tarragon for a sharp accompaniment for a dish of baked parsnips.

Unlike switching on the oven, lighting the stove means supper can be on its way in minutes. I light the stove, get out a deep pan, and fry mushrooms till golden; I boil ribbons of pasta till tender then toss the two together with cream, grated parmesan, and chopped herbs, and I have the supper of my dreams in minutes. We can't really ask for more than that.

EGGPLANT, TOMATO, COCONUT MILK

Silky eggplants. Soft spice.

Serves 4 with rice

garlic 4 cloves
ginger 1½ oz/40g
red chile 1 large
small eggplants 1 lb 8 oz/700g
peanut oil ¼ cup/60ml
ground cumin 4 teaspoons
ground coriander 4 teaspoons

garam masala 4 teaspoons
ground chile 2 teaspoons
assorted tomatoes 1 lb 2 oz/500g
uncooked strained tomatoes
 (tomato passata) 1 cup/240ml
coconut milk 2 cups/480ml
cilantro leaves a handful

Peel and finely slice the garlic, then peel and finely chop the ginger. Cut the chile into fine slices. Cut the eggplants in half.

Warm the peanut oil in a deep pan, add the garlic, ginger, and chile and allow to sizzle for a few seconds, then add the eggplants, cut side down. As the eggplants start to brown, add the cumin, coriander, garam masala, and ground chile and continue cooking for two minutes.

Roughly chop and add the tomatoes, let them soften for a couple of minutes, then pour in the passata and bring to a boil. Lower the heat and stir in the coconut milk and a generous grinding of salt. Let the ingredients bubble quietly together for a good ten minutes, until the eggplants are soft enough to crush with a spoon, then serve with a little chopped cilantro if you wish.

• Basmati rice is a fine accompaniment to this. Wash the rice in warm water, then cook in a small pan under a tight lid, with enough water to cover the grains by 1¼ inches/3cm, for ten minutes. Remove from the heat and let rest, still covered by its lid, for ten minutes before fluffing up with a fork. A few cloves, green cardamom pods, and a stick of cinnamon would be my preferred seasonings, added at the beginning of cooking.

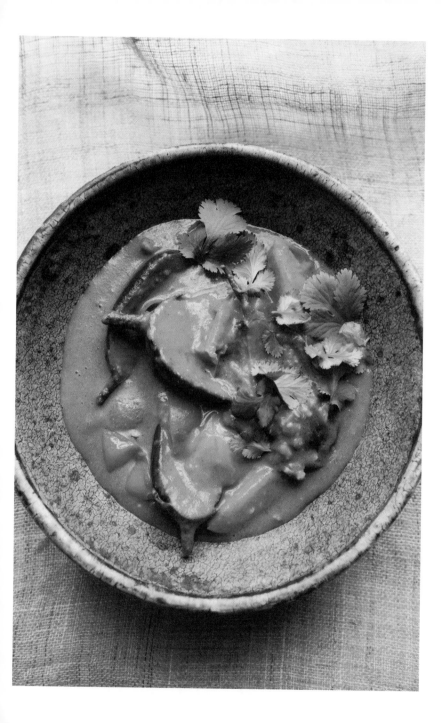

CARROTS, RICE, CILANTRO

Soft rice. Sweet, earthy flavors.

Serves 4
For the soup:
carrots 14 oz/400g
cilantro, leaves and stems
   ½ cup/10g
butter 2 tablespoons
a large shallot
garlic 2 cloves
olive oil 3 tablespoons

arborio rice 1¼ cups/250g
vegetable stock 2½ cups/600ml

To finish:
carrot 1 large
olive oil 2 tablespoons
cilantro leaves a small handful

Make the soup: Peel and roughly chop the carrots. Bring two cups/half a liter of lightly salted water to a boil in a deep pan, add the carrots, then cook for fifteen minutes or so, till tender. Put the carrots and their liquid into a blender with the cilantro and butter and process to a smooth purée.

Peel and finely chop the shallot and garlic. Warm the olive oil in a deep-sided frying pan, add the shallot and garlic, then let it cook over moderate heat for three or four minutes till fragrant, then add the rice. Ladle in the stock, a little at a time, stirring almost constantly. Continue cooking for fifteen to twenty minutes until the stock has been absorbed and the rice is tender but not soft.

Stir the puréed carrots into the rice and simmer for five minutes, then add ground black pepper and salt. To finish, peel and very finely dice the large carrot. Warm the olive oil in a pan and add the carrot. Cook for three or four minutes till the carrot is approaching tenderness. Finely chop the cilantro then spoon the soup into dishes or plates and scatter the diced carrots and cilantro.

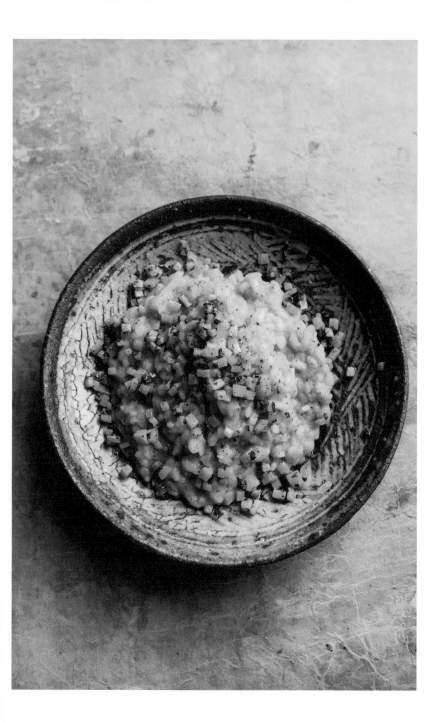

FREGOLA, GREENS, PECORINO

The smoky flavors of mushrooms and greens.

Serves 2

dried mushrooms scant 1 oz/25g
greens such as lacinato kale
   7 oz/200g

Pecorino 7 oz/200g
fregola 1 cup/200g
butter 1½ tablespoons

Bring 1 quart/1 liter of water to a boil, add the dried mushrooms, remove from the heat, and cover with a lid. Set aside for fifteen minutes to infuse.

Wash and finely shred the kale. Finely grate the Pecorino. Bring the mushroom stock back to a boil, add the fregola, and cook for twelve to fifteen minutes until tender but not soft. The pasta should still have a slight chewy quality. Drain the fregola and mushrooms.

Melt the butter in a frying pan and add the shredded greens, frying them for a minute or two till they start to brighten and wilt. Fold in the drained pasta and mushrooms, then the grated Pecorino. Pile into shallow dishes.

• Fregola is easy to find in Italian food stores. I like to look out for the Sardinian toasted variety, which has a pleasing nutty flavor.
• In place of lacinato kale, you could use crinkly-leaved Savoy cabbage or young kale.
• The quantity of Pecorino sounds alarming, but it is there to bring the whole dish together and offer a luxurious contrast to the otherwise humble ingredients.

GNOCCHI, PEAS, EGG YOLK

Hot stock, green peas, and the allure of dumplings.

Serves 2

gnocchi 14 oz/400g

vegetable stock 2 cups/480ml

frozen peas 2⅓ cups/350g

egg yolks 2

parmesan, grated
4 tablespoons/30g

Bring a deep pot of water to a boil and salt it generously. Add the gnocchi and let them cook for three or four minutes, until they come to the surface, or follow the instructions on the package. Bring the stock to a boil and add the peas.

Remove the gnocchi with a slotted spoon and divide between two bowls. Ladle in the stock and peas, then lower an egg yolk into each bowl. Sprinkle two tablespoons of grated parmesan over each serving. Stir the yolk into the stock and peas as you eat, making an impromptu sauce.

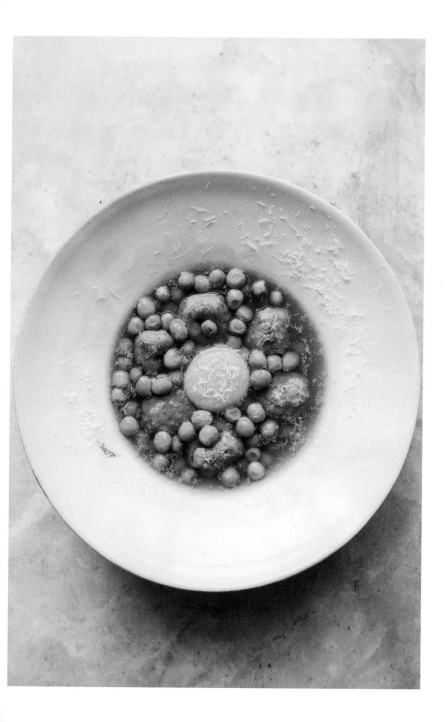

NAVY BEANS, RICE, ONIONS

A dinner of quiet sustenance.

Serves 2

onions, medium 2
olive oil 3 tablespoons
garlic a clove
white long-grain rice ¾ cup/150g
cloves 2
black peppercorns 6

navy beans 1 × 15-oz/400g can
butter ¼ cup/60g
cumin seeds 2 teaspoons
ground turmeric 1 teaspoon
chopped dill a handful

Peel the onions and thinly slice into rounds. Warm the olive oil in a saucepan, add the garlic, peeled and finely sliced, then add the onions and let them cook over moderate heat until they are soft and golden. Remove from the heat and take the onions out of the pan but keep the pan for later.

Wash the rice in warm water, drain, and transfer to a saucepan, then pour in enough water to cover it by ¾ inch/2cm. Salt the water, add the cloves and the peppercorns, then bring it to a boil. Lower the heat so that the rice simmers, cover the pan tightly with a lid, then let it cook for ten minutes. Turn off the heat, leave the lid in place, and allow the rice to rest for five minutes.

Drain the beans. Melt the butter in a pan (use the same one you cooked the onions in), then use it to cook the cumin seeds and turmeric for a minute or two until fragrant. Add the drained beans and continue cooking until they are hot.

Run a fork through the rice to separate the grains, check the seasoning, and remove the cloves. Stir in the dill, then divide between two bowls. Spoon in the navy beans and scatter the fried onions on top.

• Black-eyed peas, flageolet, lima beans, and chickpeas are fine too.

LENTILS, RUTABAGA, PAPRIKA

Sweet, roasted roots. The heartiness of lentils.

Serves 2

red onion 1
rutabaga 14 oz/400g
a large carrot
rosemary 4 sprigs
thyme 10 small sprigs
olive oil 5 tablespoons/75ml

paprika, hot 1 teaspoon
paprika, sweet 1 teaspoon
vegetable stock 2 cups/480ml
red lentils ½ cup/100g
small brown lentils ½ cup/100g
pappardelle 10½ oz/300g

Set the oven at 425°F/200°C. Peel the onion and cut into quarters. Peel the rutabaga and cut into ¾-inch/2cm chunks, then scrub the carrot and cut into similar-sized pieces. Put the onion, rutabaga, and carrot into a roasting pan together with the rosemary, thyme, and olive oil and turn with a large spoon to evenly coat each piece.

Roast for an hour or until the vegetables are golden brown and tender, turning every twenty minutes or so.

Tip the contents of the roasting pan into a large pot, add the paprikas, deglazing the roasting pan with the vegetable stock as you go, and add to the pot along with the rest of the stock. Add the lentils, season thoughtfully, and place on the stove at a low simmer for twenty minutes, stirring from time to time, or until the red lentils have virtually collapsed and the brown lentils are tender.

Cook the pappardelle in deep, generously salted boiling water for nine minutes or until it is cooked to your liking. Drain and toss with the lentil ragù.

• I am very fond of rutabaga, steamed and mashed with butter and black pepper, and I have used it sliced and cooked with cream and cheese with great success. Every time I cook with rutabaga I ask myself why I don't do so more often. *(continued)*

• Rutabaga responds to most of the spices and especially paprika and cumin. It makes a good mash when stirred through mashed carrots, calming the carrots' overly sweet notes.

MILK, MUSHROOMS, RICE

As soft and comforting as a cashmere blanket.

Serves 2

milk 2⅓ cups/800ml
water 7 tablespoons/100ml
dried mushrooms ¾ oz/20g
bay leaves 2
black peppercorns 10
half an onion
shallots 2

garlic 2 cloves
Grana Padano 3½ oz/100g
dill ¾ cup/15g
olive oil ¼ cup/60ml
arborio rice 2 cups/400g
butter 3 tablespoons

Pour the milk and water into a deep saucepan, add the dried mushrooms, bay, peppercorns, and onion half (peeled), and bring to a boil. Remove from the heat and set aside, covered with a lid, for about half an hour.

Peel and finely chop the shallots and the garlic. Grate the cheese and finely chop the dill.

Lift the mushrooms from the milk with a slotted spoon and finely chop them in a food processor, then return them to the milk. Discard the bay and onion.

Warm the oil in a pan, add the shallot and garlic, and cook over moderate heat till translucent but not colored. Stir in the rice, then add the mushroom milk, ladle by ladle, only adding more as each ladleful is absorbed. When all but 7 tablespoons/100ml of the milk has been used, stir in the butter and beat with a wooden spoon for one minute until the rice is thick and creamy, then add the remaining milk.

Stir in the grated cheese, then the dill.

• I admit I was skeptical when my collaborator, James, first suggested a milk-based risotto, but one taste and I was convinced. The milk increases the rice's ability to soothe and calm. The bay and onion are essential to provide a mild, savory back note.

MOGRABIA, TOMATOES, LABNEH

Earthy spice. Fruity sauce. The sustenance of carbs.

Serves 2

onions, medium 2
olive oil 3 tablespoons
mograbia or pearl couscous
    1 cup/200g
diced tomatoes 1 × 14.5-oz/
    400g can

Berbere spice mix 2 teaspoons
cherry tomatoes 7 oz/200g
tomatoes, medium-sized
    5¼ oz/150g
labneh ½ cup/120g

Peel the onions and slice them into ½-inch/1cm rings. Warm the olive oil in a shallow pan and cook the onions till deep gold and lightly caramelized — a good thirty minutes or more.

Bring a deep pot of water to a boil, rain in the mograbia, and boil for about twenty-five minutes till tender.

Put the chopped tomatoes in a deep pot, add the spice mix (it is already toasted so no need to fry), then bring to a boil, adding the cherry and medium-sized tomatoes, roughly chopped. Simmer for twenty minutes, stirring regularly, then add the drained mograbia, season generously, and continue to cook for another fifteen minutes until you have a rich, thick sauce.

Serve with the caramelized onions and a spoonful or two of labneh.

• Labneh is available in Middle Eastern stores and many large supermarkets. Should it evade you, use plain Greek yogurt.
• The canned diced tomatoes collapse into the sauce. The roughly chopped fresh tomatoes provide the main texture of the dish, while the cherry tomatoes introduce pleasing bursts of sweet-tartness.

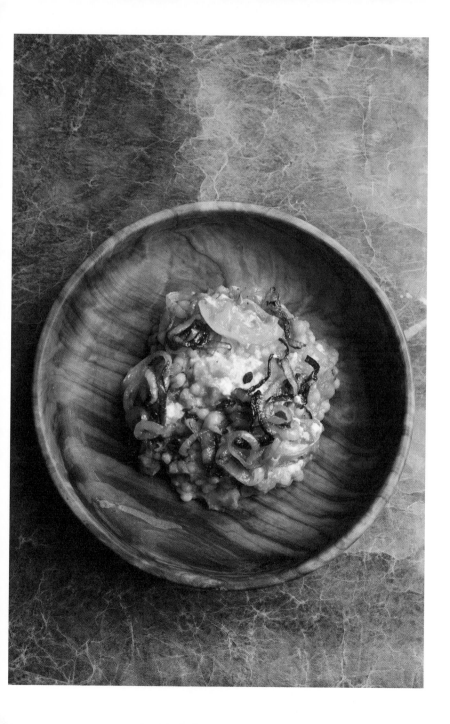

MUSHROOMS, SPINACH, RICE

Red spice, white rice. Sticky, spicy, satisfying.

Serves 2

sushi rice 1 cup/190g
warm water 1¼ cups/300ml
bay leaves 2
black peppercorns 8
roasted salted peanuts ½ cup/75g
baby spinach leaves 5 cups/100g

Thai red curry paste
  3 tablespoons
peanut oil 7 tablespoons/100ml
  plus a little extra
king oyster mushrooms 4
cilantro leaves a handful

Put the sushi rice in a medium-sized saucepan and pour the warm water over it. Set aside for half an hour.

Place the pan over moderate heat and add a half teaspoon of salt, the bay leaves, and whole black peppercorns. Bring to a boil, then lower the heat to a simmer and cover with a tight lid. Let the rice cook for twelve minutes, then remove from the heat.

Using a food processor, make a paste of the roasted salted peanuts, the washed and dried young spinach leaves, the Thai red curry paste, and 7 tablespoons/100ml of peanut oil.

Cut the king oyster mushrooms into thick slices. Warm a shallow layer of peanut oil in a frying pan, add the mushrooms and cook till golden, then turn and cook the other side. Lift half the mushrooms from the pan and drain on paper towels.

When the rice is ready, add the paste to the mushrooms left in the pan and stir for two or three minutes till the color darkens slightly. Fold in the cooked rice. Chop a small handful of cilantro leaves, fold them into the rice, then serve with the reserved drained mushrooms.

• You could use large portobello mushrooms too. Stir in more or less curry paste as the fancy takes you.

ORECCHIETTE, CAULIFLOWER, CHEESE

The reassurance of pasta. The soothing notes of cheese and cauliflower.

Serves 2

parmesan 7 oz/200g
a medium cauliflower
butter 2 tablespoons
olive oil 3 tablespoons

orecchiette 7 oz/200g
heavy cream 1 cup/240ml
dill fronds ½ cup/10g

Put a deep pot of water on to boil and salt it generously. Finely grate the parmesan. Cut the cauliflower florets from the main stalk.

Warm the butter and oil together in a shallow pan, then fry the cauliflower florets for five minutes or so until lightly crisp and golden. Put the orecchiette into the boiling water and cook for about nine minutes or until tender.

Pour the cream into the cauliflower, add the grated parmesan, and lower the heat. Drain the pasta and add it to the cauliflower and cream. Season with black pepper. Chop the dill fronds, stir into the pasta, and serve.

• Broccoli, Brussels sprouts, and kale are all perfectly acceptable in place of the cauliflower. The pasta is interchangeable too, but it's worth choosing one that will hold a little puddle of sauce, such as anelli, cavatelli, or ditalini. I suggest you avoid the larger varieties of penne, which are rather like eating pieces of rubber tubing.

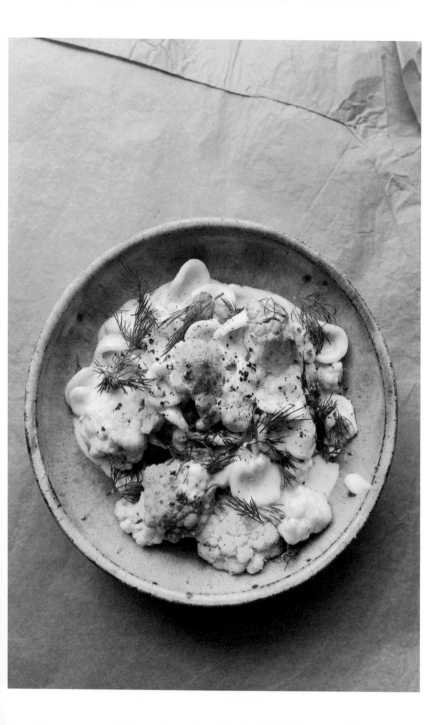

PARSNIPS, CASHEWS, SPICES

Sweet roots. Soft spice. Crunchy nuts.

Serves 2

parsnips 1 lb 2 oz/500g
onions, medium 2
garlic 2 cloves
peanut oil ¼ cup/60ml
ground turmeric 2 teaspoons
ground cumin 2 teaspoons
ground coriander 2 teaspoons

curry powder 2 teaspoons
coconut milk
    1 × 13.5-oz/400ml can
baby spinach 10 cups/200g
roasted cashews ½ cup/75g
a red chile, mild

Peel the parsnips and cut them into large pieces. Peel and roughly chop the onions. Peel and finely chop the garlic.

Warm the oil in a large, deep saucepan, add the parsnips and onions, and sauté for fifteen to twenty minutes till lightly colored, stirring regularly, then add the garlic. Fry briefly, then sprinkle in the ground spices and curry powder and continue cooking for a minute or two till fragrant. Pour in the coconut milk, bring to a boil, then lower the heat.

Wash the spinach, then put the still-wet leaves into a saucepan and cover tightly with a lid. Cook over high heat for a minute or two till the leaves wilt. Remove from the pan and squeeze dry. In a blender, process the spinach leaves with the cashews and the chile, and stir into the curry. Check the seasoning and serve.

• Much earthy sweetness here. The chile adds a kick but not so much as to mask the dish's soothing qualities.
• I do think rice is called for here and quite plain rice too. Salt, lemon zest, and maybe some chopped cilantro is all the seasoning it requires.

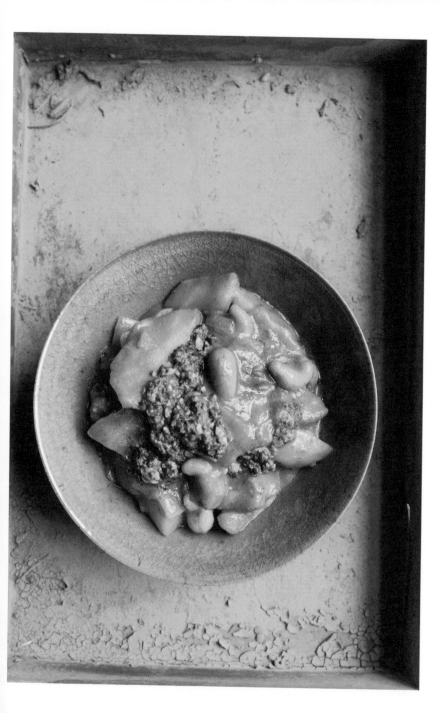

PEARL BARLEY, KALE, GOAT CHEESE

Nutty grains, melting cheese, tender greens.

Serves 2

vegetable stock 3⅓ cups/800ml
pearl barley 1 cup/200g
smoked garlic 1 head

curly kale 5¼ oz/150g
olive oil ¼ cup/60ml
goat cheese 7 oz/200g

Heat the stock in a deep pot and tip in the pearl barley. Cut the smoked garlic in half horizontally, slicing through the skin and cloves, drop into the stock, and simmer for thirty-five minutes till the barley is tender.

Cut the stems from the kale, setting the leaves aside. Roughly chop the stems. Pile the leaves on top of each other and finely shred into ribbons. Remove the smoked garlic, scoop out the flesh with a knife, and crush to a paste. Discard the skins. (Any cloves that have fallen in the barley during cooking can be left in.)

Heat the olive oil in a large, shallow pan, add the chopped kale stems, and cook for a few minutes till tender and bright. Stir in the crushed smoked garlic, then add the shredded kale leaves. Sizzle for a couple of minutes then fold into the pearl barley, together with the crumbled goat cheese.

• I have suggested kale because of its stridency against the soft, smoky grain, but almost any brassica is applicable here.
• Mozzarella would add strings of cheesy joy to the barley, as would Fontina.
• I like the nutty quality of pearl barley but this recipe could also be made with orzo pasta for a softer consistency.

POLENTA, GARLIC, MUSHROOMS

Soupy, starchy, comforting. Food to soothe and strengthen.

Serves 2–3
vegetable stock 1 quart/1 liter
coarse polenta (bramata)
  1 cup/150g
butter 6 tablespoons/80g
heavy cream 1 cup/240ml
grated parmesan 1 cup/100g

For the mushrooms:
large portobello mushrooms 2
brown button mushrooms
  5¼ oz/150g
olive oil 5 tablespoons/75ml
butter 6 tablespoons/80g
garlic 3 cloves
parsley, chopped 2 heaped
  tablespoons
chopped sage leaves 4

Bring the stock to a boil in a deep-sided, heavy-bottomed saucepan. As the stock starts to boil, rain in the polenta, stirring all the time with a wooden spoon. Continue stirring, making sure to get deep into the corners of the pan. Continue cooking, turning the heat down a little, for forty minutes, stirring almost constantly.

Cut all the mushrooms into slices about ½ inch/1cm thick. Warm the oil in a large frying pan, then add 6 tablespoons/80g of butter. When the oil starts to fizz, add the mushrooms. You may find it easier to do this in two batches. Cook the mushrooms until soft and honey-colored, turning them once during cooking, then transfer them to a dish using kitchen tongs. Don't wash the frying pan just yet.

Stir the remaining 6 tablespoons/80g of butter, the cream, and the parmesan into the polenta, then pour in enough boiling water to give a soft texture that will fall easily from the spoon. Peel and finely slice the garlic, then add to the frying pan used for the mushrooms, letting it
(continued)

brown lightly in the leftover butter. Return the mushrooms briefly to the pan, add the chopped parsley and sage, and make sure everything is hot.

Spoon the polenta into a serving dish, add the mushrooms and garlic, and serve.

• Of the two main sorts of polenta, I like to use the coarse (bramata) here. The finer version will work, but the consistency is less satisfying and produces a thinner result.
• You can omit the sage leaves if you wish — it is hardly the most useful herb to have in the house — but I often add just a few of them to polenta and, sometimes, to mashed potato.

POLENTA, THYME, TALEGGIO

Crunchy carbs. Melting Taleggio.

Serves 3-4

water 3¼ cups/750ml
coarse polenta (bramata)
   ¾ cup/125g
thyme leaves 1 teaspoon

oil, for deep frying
crème fraîche ¼ cup/60g
Taleggio 5¼ oz/150g

Bring the water to a boil in a heavy-bottomed, deep-sided pot and salt generously. Add the polenta in a continuous stream, then lower the heat and stir regularly for thirty minutes until you have a thick porridge. Stir in the thyme. Scoop the polenta into a loaf pan, approximately 8 × 5 inches/20 × 12cm, lined with plastic wrap, smooth the surface, and wrap the plastic over the top. Let cool for an hour or so.

Unwrap the polenta and turn out onto a chopping board or plate. Break into about twenty-four pieces, each one about 1-1¼ oz/30-35g in weight. The rougher the break, the more interesting the texture will be when they are fried.

Heat the oil to 355°F/180°C in a deep pot. Lower the pieces of polenta into the hot oil, one or two at a time, taking care not to overcrowd the pan. Let the polenta pieces cook for five or six minutes, turning from time to time, then remove with a slotted spoon as soon as they are crisp and golden. Place on paper towels.

Warm the crème fraîche in a heatproof bowl over a pot of simmering water. Add the cheese (cut into small pieces) and let it melt. Stir gently.

Serve the crisp pieces of polenta with the Taleggio cream.

• A crisp salad on the side. Curls of frisée crisped in iced water; white chicory and watercress would be my preference.

RICE, BROCCOLINI, BOK CHOY

The calmness of rice. The vibrancy of greens.

Serves 2

white basmati rice ⅔ cup/125g
cloves 4
bay leaves 2
green cardamom pods 6
whole black peppercorns 8
bok choy 3½ oz/100g
green onions 3

Broccolini 7 oz/200g
olive oil 2 tablespoons
five-spice powder 1 teaspoon
nigella seeds 2 teaspoons
toasted sesame oil 2 teaspoons
soy sauce to taste

Put the basmati in a mixing bowl, cover with warm water, and run your fingers through it until the water becomes cloudy. Repeat twice, until the water is almost clear. Put the rice into a small saucepan with a lid, pour in enough water to cover it by 1¼ inches/3cm, then add the cloves, bay, cardamoms lightly cracked, the peppercorns, and a half teaspoon of salt.

Bring to a boil, then cover tightly with a lid and lower the heat so the steam barely lifts the lid. Cook for ten minutes, then take off the heat and set aside without removing the lid.

Finely shred the bok choy and the green onions. Cut the Broccolini into small pieces. Warm the oil in a shallow pan that doesn't stick and add the bok choy, green onions, and Broccolini, frying till bright green and tender. Stir in the five-spice powder, nigella, and sesame oil then fluff the rice up with a fork and fold into the greens.

Spoon the rice and greens onto plates, then trickle with soy sauce.

• In place of the Broccolini, use shredded Brussels sprouts, lacinato kale, or Savoy cabbage.
• This is a useful way to use leftover rice. Add the spices and heat the rice gently and thoroughly in a wide frying pan. Continue with the recipe.

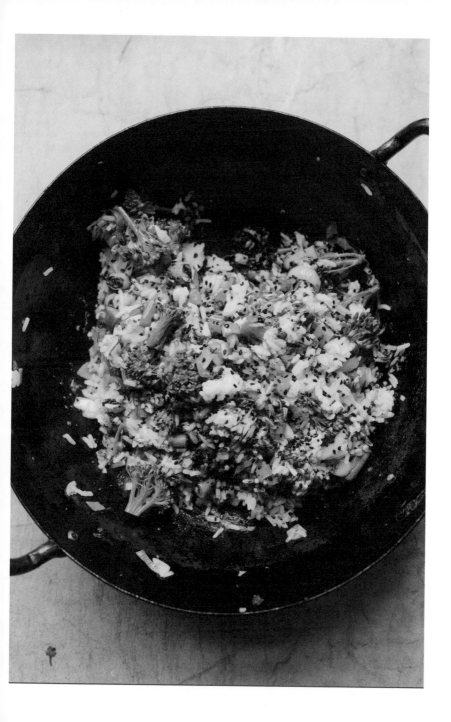

RICE, LEMON, LIME

Warm rice. A whiff of citrus.

Serves 4 as a side dish
white basmati rice 1¼ cups/250g
green cardamom pods 12
black peppercorns 10
bay leaves 2
cloves 4

lime leaves 6
a lime
a lemon
a small orange

Tip the rice into a large, wide bowl, cover with warm water, and move the grains around with your hand until the water turns milky. Drain off the water, then fill the bowl with more warm water and repeat. Do this a total of three times or until the water is almost clear. Tip the drained rice into a medium-sized saucepan.

Lightly crack the cardamom pods and add to the rice together with the whole black peppercorns, the bay leaves, cloves, and lime leaves. Grind in a half teaspoon of sea salt and pour in enough water to cover the grains by ¾ inch/2cm. Bring the water to a boil, then lower the heat and cover with a tight lid. Allow the rice to putter away for ten minutes, then remove from the heat and let rest for ten minutes, lid in place.

Finely grate the zest from the lime, lemon, and orange, making sure not to include any white pith. Remove the lid from the rice, run the tines of a fork through the grains to separate them, then fold in the grated citrus zest and a generous grinding of black pepper.

• Sometimes, all that is required is a bowl of rice. This is often lunch for me, with a cup of miso soup.

SWEET POTATO, COCONUT MILK, CASHEWS

Sweet and milky, with deep spice notes. Food to warm the soul.

Serves 4 with roti or rice

sweet potatoes 1 lb 5 oz/600g
small, waxy potatoes 14 oz/400g
sunflower oil 2 tablespoons
green cardamom pods 15
cumin seeds 2 teaspoons
ground cinnamon 1 teaspoon
ground coriander 2 teaspoons
garlic 4 cloves
small, hot red chiles 4

lemongrass 2 stalks
ginger 1¼ oz/35g
a lime
peanut oil 2 tablespoons
cashews ½ cup/75g
coconut milk 1 × 13.5-oz/
    400ml can
cilantro leaves a handful

Peel the sweet potatoes and wipe the waxy ones, then cut each into ¾-inch/2cm dice. Warm the oil in a shallow pan, then lightly brown the vegetables. They should be tender.

Crack the cardamom pods and remove the seeds, then put them in a spice mill or coffee grinder with the cumin, ground cinnamon, and ground coriander and grind everything to a powder.

Peel the garlic, roughly chop the chiles, finely slice the lemongrass, and peel and coarsely grate the ginger. Finely grate the zest from the lime and squeeze the juice. Put all into the bowl of a food processor together with the ground spices, peanut oil, and cashews. Process to a thick paste.

Put four tablespoons of the paste in a nonstick frying pan and cook over moderate heat for two or three minutes till fragrant and slightly darker in color. Stir constantly to prevent it from sticking. Stir in the coconut milk and cilantro leaves and simmer for three to four minutes, stirring almost constantly.

Divide the vegetables among four plates and spoon on some of the sauce. *(continued)*

• This is a massaman-style curry, with the richness of cashews. I marginally prefer soft, warm naan to rice to scoop this up, but either will do the trick. I really think it is worth warming the bread; in fact I would suggest it is essential. Cold naan is a friend to no one.

• Curries such as this can be made with other vegetables too. I particularly like to use plump brown button mushrooms cut into quarters before sautéing, perhaps mixed with halved Brussels sprouts.

TAGLIATELLE, DILL, MUSHROOMS

Autumn mushrooms, ribbons of pasta, a breath of aniseed.

Serves 2

dill 1¼ cups/25g
grated parmesan 1¼ cups/125g
heavy cream 1 cup/240ml
king oyster mushrooms
   7 oz/200g
small brown mushrooms
   5¼ oz/150g

chanterelles or other wild
   mushrooms 1 oz/30g
butter 2 tablespoons
olive oil 3 tablespoons
tagliatelle or fettuccine
   8 oz/250g

In a blender or food processor, reduce the dill and parmesan to fine crumbs. Tip into a saucepan, add the cream, and bring gently to a boil, stirring until the cheese melts. Cover with a lid, remove from the heat, and set aside.

Slice the oyster mushrooms into pieces about ⅛ inch/3mm thick. Clean and trim the other mushrooms. Melt the butter in the oil in a shallow pan over moderate heat. Sauté the king oyster mushrooms for three or four minutes till tender, then add the remaining mushrooms and cook for three minutes or so.

Bring a deep pot of water to a boil, salt generously, then add the pasta and let it cook till al dente. Drain, return to the pan, then fold in the cream, herb, and cheese mixture, followed by the cooked mushrooms. Divide between plates.

TOMATO, CHILES, UDON

Fruity, frugal, and a little fiery.

Serves 2

cherry tomatoes 1 lb 2 oz/500g
garlic 4 cloves
a large red chile
peanut oil 3 tablespoons

udon noodles 8 oz/250g
rice vinegar 1 tablespoon
mirin 2 teaspoons
cilantro leaves a handful

Heat the broiler to high. Halve the cherry tomatoes, peel and thinly slice the garlic, and cut the chile into very thin rounds. Put the tomatoes, garlic, and chile into a shallow roasting pan, then toss with the peanut oil. Let the tomatoes cook under the broiler till some of the skins have blackened.

Bring a deep pot of water to a boil and salt it generously. Lower the noodles into the water and let them boil for three or four minutes, or according to the instructions on the package. Drain the noodles as soon as they are tender.

Crush the tomatoes with a fork or vegetable masher, then stir in the rice vinegar, mirin, and cilantro, toss with the noodles, and serve in shallow bowls.

• Letting the tomato skins blacken under the broiler lends a smoky note to the sauce.
• I sometimes stir a little chile paste into this too, usually the tearfully hot Korean gochujang.

DESSERT

Sometimes we need dessert. A crisp-crusted tart, a slice of warm cake, or crumble-topped fruit.

Dessert can be as straightforward as a disk of shortbread, its surface studded with crushed hazelnuts and spread generously with cream and sliced blood oranges. You could finish your dinner with meringue, crushed and stirred into whipped cream, the white depths trickled with bubbling mincemeat or a sauce of hot fruit preserves.

Crumbles can be made with the usual butter, flour, and sugar crust or with breadcrumbs, butter, and syrup. That crust can shelter apples or plums, and can take ground nuts or chips of dark chocolate. It can be served hot from the oven, or chilled for breakfast. (There is actually very little difference between muesli with stewed apple and an Apple Brown Betty.)

Some like to end their meal with chocolate. In which case a dish of chocolate pudding, almost liquid in texture, to eat with a small spoon or scoop from the dish with crisp Italian cookies, may be just the thing. Others may go for broke with clusters of dried fruit held together with dark chocolate and ground pistachios.

Most of my favorite sweet treats are fruit-based. Apples are roasted and crushed, then stirred through with toasted rye crumbs and dried fruit. Bananas baked with maple syrup and puff pastry. A salad of papaya marinated in the juice of passion fruit.

There are a few that could be filed under cheating. (Whatever that means.) In particular, the idea of using premade cake in the style of a trifle, served with a pitcher of cream or, better still, a "custard" of cream and crushed cardamoms.

I will eat ice cream whatever the weather, but once the evenings draw in I am likely to serve it with melted chocolate or a glass of sherry. Then there are the confections — meringue with cream, crushed cookies or nougat or macaroons to scatter over the frost-cold surface. Whatever the weather, there must almost always be dessert.

APPLES, CINNAMON, PUFF PASTRY

Warm spice. Crisp pastry.

Makes 12

sharp "cooking" apples
   (like granny smith)
   1½ pounds 750g
pumpkin pie spice 2 teaspoons
ground cinnamon 1 teaspoon

marzipan 9 oz/250g
defrosted puff pastry
   1 (8½ oz/245g) sheet
a little beaten egg
a little ginger syrup or honey

Set the oven at 450°F/200°C. Line a baking sheet with parchment paper.

Peel and core the apples, then roughly chop half of them and put them in a deep saucepan with a splash of water. Bring to a boil, lower the heat, and let them simmer until they are soft, frothy, and can be crushed with a fork. Remove from the heat.

Cut the remaining apples into small cubes and fold them into the crushed apple with the pumpkin pie spice and ground cinnamon. This will create a nice contrast of textures.

Roll the pastry out to a rectangle measuring 14 × 9 inches/35 × 23cm. Turn the pastry so the longest edge is facing you. Cut the marzipan into tiny cubes. Spread the apple over the pastry, leaving a 1¼-inch/3cm rim on the left- and right-hand edges, then scatter the marzipan.

Brush the bare pastry rim with a little of the beaten egg. Roll the pastry up from right to left, press the egg-brushed edges firmly to seal, then cut the roll of pastry into twelve equal slices. Place the slices cut side up on the parchment-lined baking sheet.

Bake in the preheated oven for fifteen minutes, then remove from the oven and brush with a little ginger syrup or honey.

APPLES, GINGER CAKE, CUSTARD

Wobbling custard. Soft, spiced cake.

Serves 4–5
sweet apples 12¼ oz/350g
butter 3 tablespoons
plain ginger cake, store-
  bought 12¼ oz/350g
a little demerara sugar

For the custard:
eggs, large 4
heavy cream 2 cups/480ml
whole milk ½ cup/120ml
granulated sugar ¼ cup/50g
ground cinnamon a pinch
nutmeg for grating

You will need a baking dish approximately 9 inches/23cm in diameter. Set the oven at 400°F/190°C.

Quarter the apples, remove their stems and cores, then slice each quarter into three. Melt the butter in a shallow pan over moderate heat, then add the apples and let them cook for eight to ten minutes till they start to soften. Turn them over carefully with an offset spatula and continue cooking till soft.

Make the custard: break the eggs into a mixing bowl and beat with a whisk to mix whites and yolks. Pour in the cream and milk, add the granulated sugar, ground cinnamon, and a little grated nutmeg, combine thoroughly, then pour into the dish.

Crumble the ginger cake into large lumps and scatter over the custard. Add the apple slices, then sprinkle lightly with the demerara sugar. Bake for thirty-five to forty minutes till the custard is lightly set. It should wobble a little as you shake the dish. Let settle for fifteen minutes. Serve warm, though I should add it is good thoroughly chilled, too.

APPLES, OATS, CHOCOLATE

Deep, tender apple. Dark chocolate. Crisp oats.

Serves 4

sharp "cooking" apples (like granny smith) 2 lb/1kg
water 3 tablespoons
butter 2 tablespoons

For the crust:
soft, fresh white breadcrumbs ¾ cup/60g

rolled oats ⅔ cup/60g
dark chocolate chips ⅓ cup plus 1 tablespoon/70g
butter 5 tablespoons/70g
maple syrup 2 tablespoons
light brown sugar 2 tablespoons

You will need an ovenproof dish approximately 9 × 6 inches/23 × 15cm.

Set the oven at 400°F/190°C. Peel, core, and roughly chop the apples, then put them into a saucepan with the water and the 2 tablespoons of butter and cook over moderate heat for ten minutes or so, till the apples are turning to fluff. Transfer to the ovenproof dish.

Mix together the soft breadcrumbs, oats, and chocolate chips. Melt the butter and maple syrup together in a small saucepan. Scatter the crumbs over the apples, then pour in the syrup and butter, soaking the crumbs as you go.

Sprinkle the sugar on top and bake for twenty-five to thirty minutes till crisp and light gold in color.

APPLES, PEARS, RYE

Soft apples. Crisp crumbs.

Serves 4–6
sweet apples, large 4
pears, large 3
cloves 6
ground cinnamon 2 teaspoons
an orange
granulated sugar ¼ cup/50g
a lemon
butter ¼ cup/50g

For the crust:
dark rye bread 3½ oz/100g
golden raisins 6 tablespoons/55g
pumpkin pie spice 2 teaspoons
butter ¼ cup/50g
fresh cranberries 2 tablespoons

Set the oven at 425°F/200°C. Peel two of the apples, core them, and cut them into thick segments, then do the same with two of the pears. Put the peeled apples and pears in a baking dish and add the cinnamon. Remove six strips of orange peel with a vegetable peeler and tuck among the fruit.

Cut the remaining fruit into segments, coring them as you go but without peeling them, then put them into a second, smaller pan. Scatter both roasting pans of fruit with the sugar. Halve the lemon and squeeze its juice over, then dot the butter among the fruit. Bake both pans for forty-five to fifty minutes until all is soft.

Crumble the dark rye bread into a bowl and stir in the raisins and pumpkin pie spice. Melt the butter in a small pan, add the crumbled rye bread, and toast over moderate heat till lightly crisp. Set aside.

Take the pan of peeled fruit from the oven. Remove the orange peel and spices, then crush the fruit with a vegetable masher and place in a serving dish. Scatter the cranberries over the pears and apples still in the oven. When the fruit is golden and sticky and the cranberries are starting to burst, remove them from the oven. Spoon the roasted fruit over the purée, then scatter with the toasted rye bread.

BANANAS, BUTTER, PUFF PASTRY

Crisp pastry. Warm banana. The scent of maple syrup.

Makes 4

defrosted puff pastry 4½ oz/125g

butter 3 tablespoons

bananas 2

confectioners' sugar

2 tablespoons

maple syrup ¼ cup/60ml

You will need two baking sheets.

Set the oven at 450°F/220°C. Place one of the baking sheets upside down in the oven and line the other with parchment paper.

Roll the pastry thinly into a rectangle large enough from which to cut four disks of pastry 5 inches/12cm in diameter. Using a large cookie cutter or small plate as a template, cut out the four disks and transfer them to the parchment-lined baking sheet. Melt the butter in a small saucepan and slice the banana into ⅛-inch/3mm-thick pieces.

Divide the banana slices among the pieces of pastry, placing them, overlapping, in the center of the disks of pastry. Brush the bananas and pastry with melted butter, then sift the sugar over them.

Place the baking sheet on top of the hot sheet already in the oven and bake for about eighteen minutes until the pastry is golden. Spoon the maple syrup over the tarts and return to the oven for five minutes. Remove from the baking sheet with an offset spatula or fish spatula.

• Very finely sliced apples will work in place of the bananas, though they do need to be thoroughly basted with butter before baking. My favorite for this treatment is fresh apricots (they need to be exceptionally ripe), and I should perhaps mention that the canned variety, for which I retain a certain affection, are perfect candidates for a spot of high-speed baking.

(continued)

• Little tarts such as these benefit from singed edges. The contrast of the almost burned pastry with the sweet fruit and fridge-cold cream is a delight in the way of a tarte Tatin. That said, it is worth keeping a close eye on the tarts during their time in the oven. Once the pastry is brushed with syrup and returned to the oven, it will be ready in the blink of an eye.

• The frozen sheets of pre-rolled all-butter puff pastry are the ones to look out for. Let the puff pastry thaw overnight in the refrigerator.

CHOCOLATE, DRIED FRUIT, PISTACHIOS

Chewy chocolate clusters.

Makes 6
dark chocolate 3½ oz/100g
soft dried prunes 2¼ oz/60g
dried apricots 2¼ oz/60g
skinned hazelnuts mounded
    ¼ cup/40g
golden raisins ¼ cup/40g

For the pistachio sugar:
shelled pistachios 2 tablespoons
mint leaves 10
granulated sugar 1 tablespoon

Line a baking sheet with parchment paper. Break the chocolate into a heatproof bowl, place over a small saucepan of simmering water, and let melt. Try to avoid stirring; just occasionally push any unmelted pieces into the liquid chocolate. Remove the bowl from the heat.

Roughly chop the prunes and apricots. I like to slice them into small strips, each slightly thicker than a match. Roughly chop the hazelnuts, then add to the chocolate with the apricots, prunes, and raisins and stir lightly.

Place large spoonfuls of the chocolate-coated fruit and nuts on the parchment-lined baking sheet.

Put the pistachios, mint leaves, and sugar into the bowl of a food processor and blitz to a fine and pale green powder. Sprinkle over the chocolate clusters and let chill in the fridge until set.

CHOCOLATE, DULCE DE LECHE, BISCOTTI

Fragile crust. Oozing chocolate.

Serves 2

dark chocolate 3½ oz/100g
dulce de leche 2 tablespoons
eggs, large 2

granulated sugar ½ cup/100g
biscotti, to serve

Set the oven at 350°F/160°C. Break the chocolate into small pieces and allow to melt, without stirring, in a heatproof bowl suspended over a pot of simmering water. Gently stir in the dulce de leche and turn off the heat.

Break the eggs into a large bowl, add the sugar and beat until thick and fluffy. Doing this in a stand mixer with a whisk attachment will give the best results. Stir the chocolate and dulce de leche into the mixture.

Transfer to two ramekins using a rubber spatula. Put the ramekins into a roasting pan or baking dish. Pour in enough boiling water to come halfway up the sides of the ramekins, then bake for twenty minutes until the surface is lightly crisp and the inside is thick and creamy.

Serve with a small spoon and, if you wish, biscotti.

• You need only two or three stirs to incorporate the dulce de leche into the chocolate. Any more and you might overmix it.
• A soft crust appears on these puddings as you bake them, while the inside stays rich and fondant-like. It will stay like that for an hour or two, should you wish to make them a little ahead of time.
• Heatproof ceramic ramekins are ideal for these, but you can bake them in ovenproof cups too, or even metal thali dishes.
• I have baked these chocolate puddings and eaten them the following day, when they are like thick, fudgy chocolate mousse.

CHOCOLATE, ORANGE ZEST, CANDIED PEEL

Warm scones, nuggets of chocolate, a spritz of orange.

Makes 12 small scones
all-purpose flour 4 cups/500g
baking powder 1 tablespoon
chilled butter 5 tablespoons/75g
granulated sugar 1 tablespoon
an orange (medium-sized)

candied orange peel 2½ oz/75g
dark chocolate 2½ oz/75g
milk 1¼ cups/300ml
a beaten egg

Set the oven at 450°F/220°C. Line a baking sheet with parchment paper.

Sift the flour and baking powder together into a large bowl. Cut the butter into small cubes, then rub into the flour with your fingertips until you have what looks like soft, fresh breadcrumbs. Stir in the sugar. Finely grate the zest from the orange into the flour, taking care not to include any of the bitter white pith underneath.

Chop the candied peel into tiny, gravel-sized pieces and add to the bowl. Chop the chocolate into small pieces, a little larger than the cubes of peel, and stir in, together with the milk, and mix to a soft but rollable dough.

Turn out onto a lightly floured board and pat into a thick round. Using a 2½-inch/6cm biscuit cutter, cut out twelve scones and place them, a little ways apart, on the baking sheet. Brush the tops, but not the sides, of the scones with a little of the beaten egg and bake for twelve to fourteen minutes till golden. Transfer the scones to a cooling rack and serve slightly warm.

• Try to buy candied peel in large pieces. It is by far more juicy and sweet-sharp than the little nuggets you buy pre-chopped.
• Despite the chocolate, I do think these benefit from being spread with butter as you would any scone. But no cream and jam. A splodge of marmalade might be fun though.

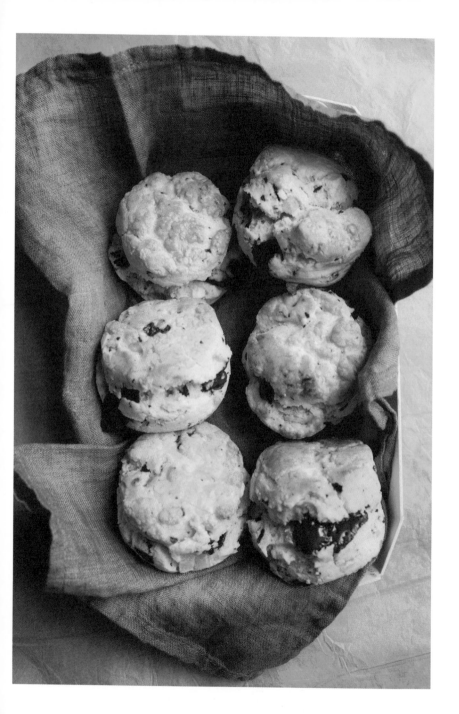

DAMSONS, ALMOND, SUNFLOWER SEEDS

Sweet homely crust. Juicy fruit.

Serves 4–6

damsons or small plums, pitted
    and quartered 1 lb 10 oz/750g
granulated sugar 2 tablespoons

For the crumble:
chilled butter 6 tablespoons/90g
all-purpose flour ⅔ cup/75g

almond meal ⅔ cup/75g
granulated sugar 3 tablespoons
salt ¼ teaspoon
sunflower seeds 3 tablespoons
lightly whipped heavy cream,
    to serve

Set the oven at 400°F/180°C. Put the damsons or plums into a baking dish approximately 8 × 9 inches/20 × 23cm. Sprinkle them lightly with the two tablespoons of sugar.

Cut the butter into small cubes, then rub into the flour and almond meal with your fingertips, until it resembles fine crumbs. Alternatively, do this using the food processor, in which case it will be done in seconds. Stir in the three tablespoons of granulated sugar, salt, and the sunflower seeds.

Shake a few drops of water over the crumble, then shake the bowl so some of the crumbs stick together in larger pieces. You get a more interesting crust that way.

Pile the crust on top of the damsons and bake for about thirty minutes until the fruit is bubbling around the edge of the crust. Serve with whipped cream.

GINGER CAKE, CARDAMOM, MAPLE SYRUP

Hot cake, spiced cream, sweet syrup.

Serves 2

heavy cream 1 cup/240ml
cardamom pods 8
granulated sugar 1 tablespoon

ginger cake, storebought
   5¼ oz/150g
butter 2 tablespoons
maple syrup 2 tablespoons

Put the cream in a small saucepan. Break open the cardamom pods and crush the seeds to powder in a spice mill or a mortar and pestle. Stir the powder into the cream, add the sugar, then simmer for three minutes and remove from the heat.

Cut the ginger cake into four slices ¾ inch/2cm thick. Warm the butter in a frying pan, add the ginger cake, and cook for a couple of minutes until thoroughly hot. Remove and divide between two dishes. Pour the cardamom cream over the ginger cake, then trickle over the maple syrup.

• I say ginger cake, but to be honest any quick bread would do. A lemon cake is good here, as are spice cakes and those made with golden syrup.
• Cardamom has an affinity with sweet baking and is I think perfect here, but you could use a little cinnamon instead if you like. You will need barely a half teaspoon.

HAZELNUTS, BLOOD ORANGES, RICOTTA

The warmth of nuts and honey. The brightness of oranges.

Serves 6
For the base:
room temperature butter ½ cup
    plus 2 tablespoons/150g
confectioners' sugar ½ cup/60g
almond meal ⅔ cup/80g
all-purpose flour ⅔ cup/75g
skinned hazelnuts ⅓ cup/50g
pine nuts ⅓ cup/40g
poppy seeds 1 tablespoon
sesame seeds 1 tablespoon
sliced almonds ¼ cup/30g

shelled pistachios ⅓ cup/40g
a small lemon
blood oranges 4
heavy cream ½ cup plus
    2 tablespoons/150ml
ricotta ¾ cup plus 1
    tablespoon/200g

For the syrup:
honey 3 tablespoons
thyme leaves 2 teaspoons

Set the oven at 350°F/160°C. Using a stand mixer fitted with the paddle attachment, cream the butter and sugar together. Fold in the almond meal and flour. Chop the hazelnuts in half, then mix with the pine nuts, poppy and sesame seeds, sliced almonds, and pistachios. Finely grate the zest from the lemon, then fold, together with the seeds and nuts, into the shortbread dough.

Bring the mixture together with floured hands, put on a parchment-lined baking sheet, then lightly pat into a rectangle roughly 9 × 10 inches/23 × 25cm. Bake for twenty to twenty-five minutes until pale cookie-colored. Remove from the oven and let cool for ten minutes, then slide carefully onto a cooling rack and let cool completely.

Remove the peel from three of the oranges with a sharp knife, then slice the fruit thinly and place in a small bowl. Put the cream in a mixing bowl and beat until thick, but not so firm it will stand in peaks. Fold in the ricotta and refrigerate. *(continued)*

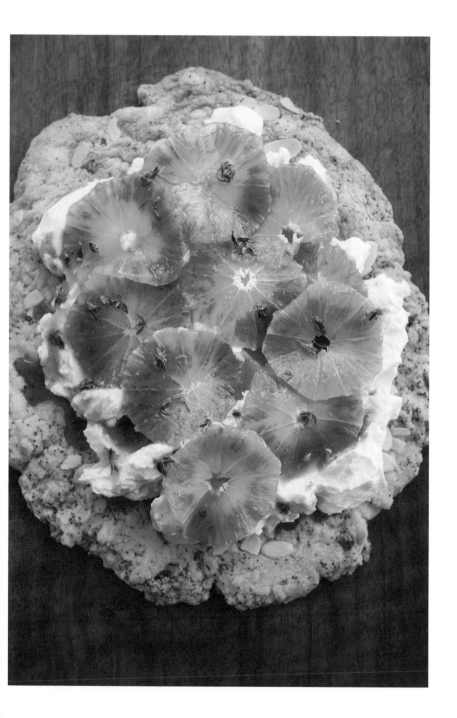

Put the juice of the fourth orange, the honey, and the thyme leaves into a small pan and warm over low heat until the honey has melted. Slide the shortbread onto a serving plate or board, spoon the chilled ricotta cream over the surface, then cover with the sliced oranges. Spoon the orange and thyme syrup over the fruit and serve.

ICE CREAM, CHOCOLATE, SHERRY

Cold ice cream. Hot chocolate sauce. The deep, sticky sweetness of sherry.

Serves 2

sliced almonds 1 tablespoon
dark chocolate 2½ oz/75g
vanilla ice cream 4 scoops

dry sherry
2 tablespoons
crystallized orange

Toast the sliced almonds in a dry, shallow pan over moderate heat till patchily golden. Take great care not to get distracted — nuts burn in seconds.

Break the chocolate into a small heatproof bowl suspended over simmering water and let melt.

Place the scoops of ice cream in two bowls, pour in the sherry, then spoon in the melted chocolate. Finish with the sliced almonds and a tiny slice of crystallized orange and eat immediately.

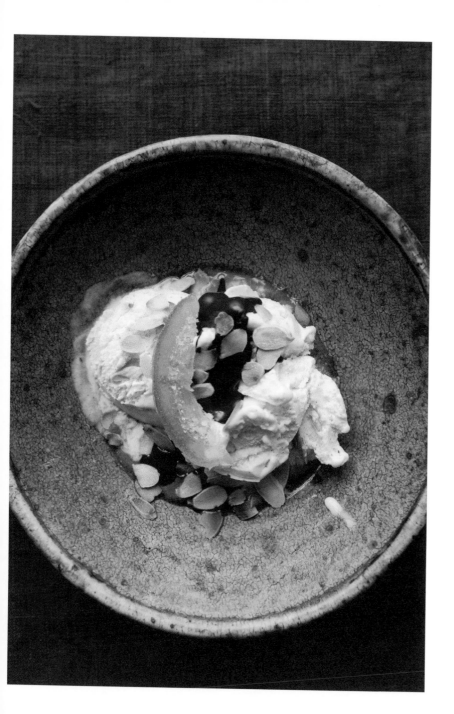

CRANBERRY, MINCEMEAT, MERINGUE

Crisp meringue. Whipped cream. Sweet mincemeat. Sour cranberries.

Serves 2

cranberries, fresh 1¼ cups/125g
cranberry jelly ½ cup/150g
heavy cream 1 cup/240ml

meringues 3 oz/80g
mincemeat scant 1 cup/200g
Marsala 3 tablespoons

Put the cranberries in a saucepan with the cranberry jelly and cook over moderate heat for five to seven minutes till the berries burst.

Pour the cream into a chilled bowl and whisk till thick. The cream should be just stiff enough to sit in soft folds. Crumble the meringues into the cream.

Warm the mincemeat and Marsala together in a small pan until they are hot and bubbling, then remove from the heat.

Divide the meringue and cream between two bowls, then spoon in the hot mincemeat followed by the hot cranberry sauce.

• You could successfully add slices of blood orange to this, too.

PAPAYA, PASSION FRUIT, MINT

Tart, bright flavors for a gray day.

Serves 4

passion fruit 6	persimmon 1
orange 1, small	papayas 2
cardamom pods 4	mint leaves 6

Slice the passion fruit in half, then squeeze their juice and seedy flesh into a small sieve over a bowl. Press the juice and pulp through the sieve with the back of a small spoon, then discard the seeds. Cut the orange in half and squeeze its juice into the bowl of passion fruit juice.

Crack open the cardamom pods with a heavy weight, such as a pestle or rolling pin, then drop them, whole, into the juice. Cover and place in the fridge.

Slice the persimmon thinly, then add to the passion fruit juice. Slice the papayas in half, scrape out the seeds with a small spoon and discard them, then remove the yellow skin from each papaya half using a vegetable peeler. Slice the papaya into thick pieces about the width of a pencil. Mix the papaya pieces with the persimmon and passion fruit juice, tossing the fruits tenderly together.

Cover and let rest for a couple of hours, or overnight, in the fridge. Add the mint leaves and remove the cardamom pods — they have done their work — then divide the fruit among four small bowls.

PEARS, RED WINE, PECORINO

Fruity, long-matured cheese, spiced fruit.

Serves 4

pears 4
star anise 2
cardamom pods 10
a vanilla pod

cloves 4
a cinnamon stick
a bottle of light, fruity red wine
aged Pecorino 12¼ oz/350g

Peel the pears and tuck them snugly into a stainless-steel saucepan. Add the star anise, cardamom pods — lightly cracked open — the vanilla pod (split in half lengthwise), and the cloves. Break the cinnamon stick in half, add to the pan, then pour in the red wine.

Bring the wine almost to a boil, lower the heat to a simmer, then let cook until the pears are tender. Expect this to take anything from twenty minutes to fifty, depending on the ripeness of your pears.

Slice the cheese, drain the pears (discarding the spices), and put them both on a serving plate.

• You can reuse the spiced red wine. Once you have removed the pears, turn the heat up, add ½ cup/100g of granulated sugar and let the wine bubble to a deep, garnet-red syrup. Keep your eye on it, but it will probably take a full ten minutes. When all is deep red and glossy, pour into a small jug and let cool. Pour over vanilla ice cream.

RICE PUDDING, ROSE WATER, APRICOTS

Creamy rice. A hint of rose water.

Serves 4

short-grain white rice
   ¾ cup/150g
heavy cream 1 cup/240ml
whole milk 1 cup/240ml
granulated sugar 2 tablespoons
a vanilla pod
rose water 2 teaspoons
orange blossom water
   2 teaspoons
pistachios, roughly chopped
   ⅓ cup/50g

rose petals, fresh or dried
   2 tablespoons

For the apricots:
water 1¼ cups/300ml
dried apricots 16
half a cinnamon stick
a lemon

Put the rice in a medium, heavy-bottomed pan, then add the cream, milk, sugar, and vanilla pod. Bring to a boil over medium heat, then turn down the heat until the milk is bubbling gently. Allow to simmer for twenty-five minutes or until tender, giving it the occasional stir.

Put the water in a medium-sized pan and add the dried apricots, cinnamon stick, and the juice and shell of the lemon. Bring to a boil, then lower the heat and simmer for ten minutes.

When the rice is soft, remove the vanilla pod and stir in the rose and orange blossom waters. Divide the rice pudding among four bowls. Spoon four apricots over each, with a little of the juice from the pan. Scatter the pistachios and a few rose petals before serving.

SHERRY, BLOOD ORANGES, CREAM

The nutty warmth of sherry. The vibrancy of oranges.

Serves 4

blood orange 1 small
lemon 1 small
dry sherry
   5 tablespoons/75ml
granulated sugar
   6 tablespoons/75g

heavy cream 1¼ cups/300ml

To finish:
dark chocolate 1¾ oz/50g
candied orange peel 2½ oz/75g
blood oranges 2

Finely grate the zest of one blood orange and the lemon into a mixing bowl. Squeeze the fruits' juice into the bowl, pour in the sherry, and stir in the sugar. Mix until the sugar has dissolved, then set aside for a good two hours or even overnight.

Make the chocolate-dipped peel. Melt the chocolate in a small heatproof bowl over a pot of simmering water, removing it from the heat as soon as the chocolate is liquid. Cut the candied peel into short pieces about ½-inch/1cm thick and the length of a matchstick. Dip each piece of peel into the chocolate, place on a piece of parchment paper, and leave in a cool place until the chocolate has set.

Pour the cream into the fruit juice and sherry, then slowly whip until the syllabub starts to thicken. It is best to whip slowly, watching the consistency of the syllabub constantly. As it starts to thicken, the cream will feel heavy on the whisk and you should stop as soon as the syllabub is thick enough to sit in soft, gentle waves. If you whisk until it will stand in peaks, you have gone too far. Keep chilled in the refrigerator.

Remove the peel from the remaining blood oranges with a very sharp knife, taking every shred of white pith with you. Slice the fruit thinly. Spoon the chilled syllabub into bowls, then add the slices of blood orange and the chocolate-dipped candied peel.

RICE, MILK, FIG JAM

The humble sweetness of baked rice. The syrupy luxury of fig preserves.

Serves 4

green cardamom pods 6
milk 1 quart/1 liter
bay leaves 2
a vanilla pod
butter 2 tablespoons

short-grain white rice
    6 tablespoons/80g
granulated sugar 3–4 tablespoons
fig jam ½ cup/150g

Set the oven at 325°F/140°C.

Crack the green cardamoms, extract the tiny brown-black seeds, then crush them to a powder. A mortar and pestle will work if you don't have a spice mill. Pour the milk into a saucepan. Add the ground cardamom, bay leaves, vanilla pod, and butter and bring to a boil.

Put the rice and sugar in a baking dish, then, as soon as the milk boils (watch carefully), pour the hot milk over the rice and stir till the sugar has dissolved.

Slide the dish into the preheated oven and bake for two hours until the rice is soft and creamy and the skin is pale gold. Serve with spoonfuls of soft fig jam.

• No effort involved here. Just a little patience.
• If fig jam proves tricky to track down, slice six small fresh figs in half and put them in a saucepan with four tablespoons each of granulated sugar and water. Bring to a boil, then lower the heat and simmer till the sugar and water have turned to a syrup and the figs are soft and on the point of collapse.

INDEX

A
almonds:
    damsons, almond, sunflower seeds 262
    hazelnuts, blood oranges, ricotta 266-8
    ice cream, chocolate, sherry 270
    red cabbage, carrots, smoked almonds 140
    (see also marzipan)
apples:
    apple yogurt 14-16
    apples, blue cheese, walnuts 134
    apples, cinnamon, puff pastry 244
    apples, ginger cake, custard 246
    apples, oats, chocolate 248
    apples, pears, rye 250
    beet, apple, goat cheese 48
    shallots, apples, parmesan 152
apricots:
    chocolate, dried fruit, pistachios 256
    rice pudding, rose water, apricots 278
artichokes, beans, green olives 12
artichokes, Jerusalem *(see Jerusalem
    artichokes)*

B
bananas, butter, puff pastry 252-4
barley:
    pearl barley, kale, goat cheese 220
bay leaves:
    cauliflower, onions, bay 82
bean sprouts:
    eggs, edamame, bean sprouts 26-8

beans:
    artichokes, beans, green olives 12
    beans, rosemary, kale 170
    burrata, beans, tomatoes 20
    chickpeas, radicchio, lima beans 90
    lima beans, peppers, eggplants 74-6
    navy beans, rice, onions 204
    noodles, lentils, sour cream 182-4
    sweet potato, jalapeño, beans 124
beet:
    artichokes, winter roots, smoked
        salt 68-70
    beet, apple, goat cheese 48
    beet, blood orange, watercress 136
    beet, lentils, garam masala 166
    beet, sauerkraut, dill 168
Berbere spice:
    cabbage, Berbere spice, crumbs 78
biscotti:
    chocolate, dulce de leche, biscotti 258
black-eyed peas:
    beans, rosemary, kale 170
    sweet potato, jalapeño, beans 124
blackberries:
    apples, blue cheese, walnuts 134
blue cheese:
    apples, blue cheese, walnuts 134
    Brussels tops, blue cheese 172
    mushrooms, blue cheese, English
        muffins 60

bok choy:
    eggs, edamame, bean sprouts 26–8
    rice, broccoli, bok choy 228
bread:
    celeriac, horseradish, pumpernickel 174
    (see also toast)
breadcrumbs:
    apples, oats, chocolate 248
    apples, pears, rye 250
    Brussels sprouts, smoked mozzarella,
        dill 72
    butternut, breadcrumbs, curry powder 22
    cabbage, Berbere spice, crumbs 78
    fennel, cream, pine nuts 92
    mushrooms, orange, breadcrumbs 138
broccoli:
    filo pastry, cheese, greens 146
    rice, broccoli, bok choy 228
Brussels sprouts:
    Brussels sprouts, brown rice, miso 18
    Brussels sprouts, smoked mozzarella,
        dill 72
    potatoes, Brussels sprouts 106
Brussels tops *(see sprout tops)*
burrata, beans, tomatoes 20
butternut squash:
    butternut, breadcrumbs, curry powder 22
    butternut, feta, eggs 24
    mushrooms, butternut, sour cream 180
    pumpkin, couscous, date syrup 118
    tahini, sesame, butternut 188–90

C

cabbage:
    cabbage, Berbere spice, crumbs 78
    (see also red cabbage)
cakes:
    apples, ginger cake, custard 246
    ginger cake, cardamom, maple syrup 264
candied peel:
    chocolate, orange zest, candied peel 260

cannellini beans:
    burrata, beans, tomatoes 20
caramel:
    chocolate, dulce de leche, biscotti 258
cardamom pods:
    ginger cake, cardamom, maple syrup 264
    papaya, passion fruit, mint 274
    pears, red wine, Pecorino 276
    rice, milk, fig jam 282
    sweet potato, coconut milk,
        cashews 232–4
carrots:
    artichokes, winter roots, smoked
        salt 68–70
    black-eyed beans, rosemary, kale 170
    a brown vegetable stock 4
    butternut, breadcrumbs, curry powder 22
    carrots, rice, cilantro 198
    carrots, spices, paneer 80
    cheddar, cider, mustard 176
    lentils, rutabaga, paprika 206–8
    parsnips, smoked garlic, feta 104
    red cabbage, carrots, smoked almonds 140
cashews:
    parsnips, cashews, spices 218
    sweet potato, coconut milk,
        cashews 232–4
cauliflower:
    cauliflower, onions, bay 82
    orecchiette, cauliflower, cheese 216
celeriac:
    artichokes, winter roots, smoked
        salt 68–70
    celeriac, horseradish, pumpernickel 174
chanterelles:
    tagliatelle, dill, mushrooms 236
chard:
    rainbow chard, egg, noodles 40
cheddar, cider, mustard 176
cheddar, tarragon, eggs 84–6

cheese:
    apples, blue cheese, walnuts 134
    beet, apple, goat cheese 48
    Brussels sprouts, smoked mozzarella,
      dill 72
    Brussels tops, blue cheese 172
    burrata, beans, tomatoes 20
    butternut, feta, eggs 24
    carrots, spices, paneer 80
    cheddar, cider, mustard 176
    cheddar, tarragon, eggs 84–6
    cheese, thyme, grapes 88
    crumpets, cream cheese, spinach 50–2
    fennel, peas, halloumi 30
    filo pastry, cheese, greens 146
    fregola, greens, Pecorino 200
    hazelnuts, blood oranges, ricotta 266–8
    leeks, Caerphilly, mustard 58
    leeks, tomato, Pecorino 150
    milk, mushrooms, rice 210
    mushrooms, blue cheese, English
      muffins 60
    naan, mozzarella, tomatoes 62
    onions, Taleggio, cream 100
    orecchiette, cauliflower, cheese 216
    orzo, smoked mozzarella, thyme 186
    parsley, parmesan, eggs 36
    parsnips, shallots, goat cheese 102
    parsnips, smoked garlic, feta 104
    pearl barley, kale, goat cheese 220
    pears, red wine, Pecorino 276
    polenta, garlic, mushrooms 222–4
    polenta, thyme, Taleggio 226
    rutabaga, mushroom, Gruyère,
      thyme 154–6
    shallots, apples, parmesan 152
    sweet potato, jalapeño, beans 124
    tagliatelle, dill, mushrooms 236
chestnuts:
    tahini, sesame, butternut 188–90
chickpeas:

chickpeas, radicchio, lima beans 90
mushrooms, chickpeas, tahini 98
mushrooms, hummus, herbs 34
noodles, lentils, sour cream 182–4
pumpkin, chickpeas, rosemary 114–16
chiles:
    eggplant, tomato, coconut milk 196
    eggs, edamame, bean sprouts 26–8
    parsnips, cashews, spices 218
    rainbow chard, egg, noodles 40
    sweet potato, coconut milk,
      cashews 232–4
    sweet potato, jalapeño, beans 124
    tomato, chiles, udon 238
chocolate:
    apples, oats, chocolate 248
    chocolate, dried fruit, pistachios 256
    chocolate, dulce de leche, biscotti 258
    chocolate, orange zest, candied peel 260
    ice cream, chocolate, sherry 270
cider:
    cheddar, cider, mustard 176
cilantro:
    carrots, rice, cilantro 198
    rainbow chard, egg, noodles 40
cinnamon:
    apples, cinnamon, puff pastry 244
coconut milk:
    eggplant, tomato, coconut milk 196
    parsnips, cashews, spices 218
    sweet potato, coconut milk,
      cashews 232–4
cookies:
    chocolate, dulce de leche, biscotti 258
couscous:
    mograbia, tomatoes, labneh 212
    pumpkin, couscous, date syrup 118
cranberries:
    apples, pears, rye 250
    cranberry, mincemeat, meringue 272

cream:
  Brussels sprouts, smoked mozzarella,
    dill 72
  cranberry, mincemeat, meringue 272
  custard 246
  fennel, cream, pine nuts 92
  ginger cake, cardamom, maple syrup 264
  hazelnuts, blood oranges, ricotta 266–8
  mushrooms, hummus, herbs 34
  onions, Taleggio, cream 100
  orecchiette, cauliflower, cheese 216
  polenta, garlic, mushrooms 222–4
  potatoes, sweet potatoes, cream 108
  rice pudding, rosewater, apricots 278
  pumpkin, mustard, cream 120–2
  sherry, blood oranges, cream 280
  (see also sour cream)
cream cheese:
  crumpets, cream cheese, spinach 50–2
crème fraîche:
  polenta, thyme, Taleggio 226
crumbles:
  apples, pears, rye 250
  damsons, almond, sunflower seeds 262
  leeks, tomato, Pecorino 150
crumpets:
  crumpets, cream cheese, spinach 50–2
  leeks, Caerphilly, mustard 58
cucumber:
  fennel, cucumber, mint 178
curry:
  beet, lentils, garam masala 166
  butternut, breadcrumbs, curry powder 22
  eggplant, tomato, coconut milk 196
  eggs, spinach, bread 54–6
  lentils, sweet potato, tomatoes 94–6
  mushrooms, spinach, rice 214
  parsnips, cashews, spices 218
  sweet potato, coconut milk,
    cashews 232–4

custard:
  apples, ginger cake, custard 246

D
damsons, almond, sunflower seeds 262
date syrup:
  oats, dried mulberries, date syrup 6
  pumpkin, couscous, date syrup 118
dal:
  beet, lentils, garam masala 166
dill:
  beet, sauerkraut, dill 168
  Brussels sprouts, smoked mozzarella,
    dill 72
  tagliatelle, dill, mushrooms 236
dried fruit:
  chocolate, dried fruit, pistachios 256
drop scones:
  parsley, parmesan, eggs 36
dulce de leche:
  chocolate, dulce de leche, biscotti 258

E
edamame beans:
  eggs, edamame, bean sprouts 26–8
eggplants:
  eggplant, tomato, coconut milk 196
  eggplants, ginger, tamarind 14–16
  lima beans, peppers, eggplants 74–6
eggs:
  butternut, feta, eggs 24
  cheddar, tarragon, eggs 84–6
  custard 246
  eggs, edamame, bean sprouts 26–8
  eggs, spinach, bread 54–6
  gnocchi, peas, egg yolk 202
  parsley, parmesan, eggs 36
  rainbow chard, egg, noodles 40

F
fennel:
    fennel, cream, pine nuts 92
    fennel, cucumber, mint 178
    fennel, peas, halloumi 30
fig jam:
    rice, milk, fig jam 282
figs:
    mushrooms, orange, breadcrumbs 138
filo pastry, cheese, greens 146
fregola, greens, Pecorino 200
fritters:
    butternut, feta, eggs 24
    polenta, thyme, Taleggio 226

G
garam masala:
    beet, lentils, garam masala 166
    eggplant, tomato, coconut milk 196
garlic:
    parsnips, smoked garlic, feta 104
    pearl barley, kale, goat cheese 220
    polenta, garlic, mushrooms 222-4
    potatoes, Brussels sprouts 106
    potatoes, tomatoes, horseradish 112
ginger:
    apples, ginger cake, custard 246
    eggplants, ginger, tamarind 14-16
    ginger cake, cardamom, maple syrup 264
gnocchi, peas, egg yolk 202
goat cheese:
    beet, apple, goat cheese 48
    parsnips, shallots, goat cheese 102
    pearl barley, kale, goat cheese 220
golden raisins:
    apples, pears, rye 250
    chocolate, dried fruit, pistachios 256
    Jerusalem artichokes, pistachios,
        grapes 32
    oats, dried mulberries, date syrup 6

grapes:
    cheese, thyme, grapes 88
    Jerusalem artichokes, pistachios,
        grapes 32

H
harissa paste:
    sweet potato, puff pastry 158-60
hazelnuts:
    chocolate, dried fruit, pistachios 256
    hazelnuts, blood oranges, ricotta 266-8
    mushrooms, orange, breadcrumbs 138
honey:
    hazelnuts, blood oranges, ricotta 266-8
horseradish:
    beet, sauerkraut, dill 168
    celeriac, horseradish, pumpernickel 174
    potatoes, tomatoes, horseradish 112
hummus:
    mushrooms, hummus, herbs 34
    pumpkin, chickpeas, rosemary 114-16

I
ice cream, chocolate, sherry 270

J
jalapeño chile:
    sweet potato, jalapeño, beans 124
Jerusalem artichokes:
    artichokes, winter roots, smoked
        salt 68-70
    Jerusalem artichokes, pistachios,
        grapes 32

K
kale:
    black-eyed beans, rosemary, kale 170
    pearl barley, kale, goat cheese 220

L

labneh:
  mograbia, tomatoes, labneh 212
lacinato kale:
  fregola, greens, Pecorino 200
leeks:
  leeks, Caerphilly, mustard 58
  leeks, parsnips, pastry 148
  leeks, tomato, Pecorino 150
lemon:
  chickpeas, radicchio, lima beans 90
  rice, lemon, lime 230
lemongrass:
  sweet potato, coconut milk,
    cashews 232-4
lentils:
  beet, lentils, garam masala 166
  lentils, rutabaga, paprika 206-8
  lentils, sweet potato, tomatoes 94-6
  noodles, lentils, sour cream 182-4
lettuce:
  apples, blue cheese, walnuts 134
lima beans:
  lima beans, peppers, eggplants 74-6
  chickpeas, radicchio, lima beans 90
lime:
  eggplants, ginger, tamarind 14-16
  rice, lemon, lime 230

M

maple syrup:
  bananas, butter, puff pastry 252-4
  ginger cake, cardamom, maple syrup 264
Marsala:
  cranberry, mincemeat, meringue 272
marzipan:
  apples, cinnamon, puff pastry 244
meringue:
  cranberry, mincemeat, meringue 272
milk:
  Brussels tops, blue cheese 172

cauliflower, onions, bay 82
celeriac, horseradish, pumpernickel 174
cheddar, cider, mustard 176
milk, mushrooms, rice 210
orzo, smoked mozzarella, thyme 186
rice pudding, rose water, apricots 278
rice, milk, fig jam 282
mincemeat:
  cranberry, mincemeat, meringue 272
mint:
  apple yogurt 14-16
  fennel, cucumber, mint 178
  papaya, passion fruit, mint 274
miso paste:
  Brussels sprouts, brown rice, miso 18
mograbia, tomatoes, labneh 212
muffins:
  mushrooms, blue cheese, English
    muffins 60
mulberries (dried):
  oats, dried mulberries, date syrup 6
mushrooms:
  leeks, parsnips, pastry 148
  milk, mushrooms, rice 210
  mushrooms, blue cheese, toasting
    muffins 60
  mushrooms, butternut, sour cream 180
  mushrooms, chickpeas, tahini 98
  mushrooms, hummus, herbs 34
  mushrooms, orange, breadcrumbs 138
  mushrooms, spinach, rice 214
  parsnips, shallots, goat cheese 102
  polenta, garlic, mushrooms 222-4
  rutabaga, mushroom, Gruyère,
    thyme 154-6
  tagliatelle, dill, mushrooms 236
mustard:
  cheddar, cider, mustard 176
  leeks, Caerphilly, mustard 58
  pumpkin, mustard, cream 120-2

N

naan, mozzarella, tomatoes 62

navy beans:
    artichokes, beans, green olives 12
    navy beans, rice, onions 204
    noodles, lentils, sour cream 182–4

noodles:
    noodles, lentils, sour cream 182–4
    rainbow chard, egg, noodles 40
    tomato, chiles, udon 238

O

oats:
    apples, oats, chocolate 248
    oats, dried mulberries, date syrup 6
    winter porridge 3

olives:
    artichokes, beans, green olives 12

omelettes:
    eggs, edamame, bean sprouts 26–8

onions:
    a brown vegetable stock 4
    cauliflower, onions, bay 82
    cheddar, cider, mustard 176
    lentils, rutabaga, paprika 206–8
    mograbia, tomatoes, labneh 212
    navy beans, rice, onions 204
    noodles, lentils, sour cream 182–4
    onions, Taleggio, cream 100
    parsnips, cashews, spices 218
    parsnips, smoked garlic, feta 104
    potatoes, sweet potatoes, cream 108
    pumpkin, onions, rosemary 38
    (see also shallots)

oranges:
    beet, blood orange, watercress 136
    chickpeas, radicchio, lima beans 90
    chocolate, orange zest, candied peel 260
    fennel, cream, pine nuts 92
    hazelnuts, blood oranges, ricotta 266–8
    mushrooms, orange, breadcrumbs 138

    papaya, passion fruit, mint 274
    rice, lemon, lime 230
    sherry, blood oranges, cream 280

orecchiette, cauliflower, cheese 216

orzo, smoked mozzarella, thyme 186

oyster mushrooms:
    mushrooms, hummus, herbs 34
    mushrooms, spinach, rice 214
    tagliatelle, dill, mushrooms 236

P

paneer:
    carrots, spices, paneer 80

papaya, passion fruit, mint 274

pappardelle:
    lentils, rutabaga, paprika 206–8

parsley, parmesan, eggs 36

parsnips:
    artichokes, winter roots, smoked
      salt 68–70
    leeks, parsnips, pastry 148
    parsnips, cashews, spices 218
    parsnips, shallots, goat cheese 102
    parsnips, smoked garlic, feta 104

passion fruit:
    papaya, passion fruit, mint 274

pasta:
    gnocchi, peas, egg yolk 202
    lentils, rutabaga, paprika 206–8
    orecchiette, cauliflower, cheese 216
    orzo, smoked mozzarella, thyme 186
    tagliatelle, dill, mushrooms 236

pastries:
    apples, cinnamon, puff pastry 244
    filo pastry, cheese, greens 146
    sweet potato, puff pastry 158–60
    (see also pies; tarts)

peanuts:
    mushrooms, spinach, rice 214

pearl barley, kale, goat cheese 220

pears:
    apples, pears, rye 250
    pears, red wine, Pecorino 276
    red cabbage, carrots, smoked almonds 140
peas:
    fennel, peas, halloumi 30
    gnocchi, peas, egg yolk 202
peppers:
    lima beans, peppers, eggplants 74-6
persimmon:
    papaya, passion fruit, mint 274
pies:
    leeks, parsnips, pastry 148
    (see also pastries; tarts)
pine nuts:
    fennel, cream, pine nuts 92
    hazelnuts, blood oranges, ricotta 266-8
pistachios:
    chocolate, dried fruit, pistachios 256
    Jerusalem artichokes, pistachios,
        grapes 32
polenta:
    artichokes, beans, green olives 12
    polenta, garlic, mushrooms 222-4
    polenta, thyme, Taleggio 226
ponzu sauce:
    tofu, radish, ponzu 42
porridge:
    oats, dried mulberries, date syrup 6
    winter porridge 3
potatoes:
    potatoes, Brussels sprouts 106
    potatoes, sweet potatoes, cream 108
    potatoes, tahini, thyme 110
    potatoes, tomatoes, horseradish 112
    sweet potato, coconut milk,
        cashews 232-4
prunes:
    chocolate, dried fruit, pistachios 256
    rice pudding, rose water, apricots 278

puff pastry:
    apples, cinnamon, puff pastry 244
    bananas, butter, puff pastry 252-4
    sweet potato, puff pastry 158-60
pumpernickel:
    celeriac, horseradish, pumpernickel 174
pumpkin:
    pumpkin, chickpeas, rosemary 114-16
    pumpkin, couscous, date syrup 118
    pumpkin, mustard, cream 120-2
    pumpkin, onions, rosemary 38
purple sprouting broccoli:
    filo pastry, cheese, greens 146

R
radicchio:
    chickpeas, radicchio, lima beans 90
radishes:
    beet, blood orange, watercress 136
    fennel, cucumber, mint 178
    sweet potato, jalapeño, beans 124
    tofu, radish, ponzu 42
rainbow chard, egg, noodles 40
red cabbage, carrots, smoked almonds 140
rice:
    Brussels sprouts, brown rice, miso 18
    carrots, rice, cilantro 198
    navy beans, rice, onions 204
    milk, mushrooms, rice 210
    mushrooms, spinach, rice 214
    rice pudding, rose water, apricots 278
    rice, broccoli, bok choy 228
    rice, lemon, lime 230
    rice, milk, fig jam 282
risotto:
    milk, mushrooms, rice 210
root vegetables:
    artichokes, winter roots, smoked
        salt 68-70
    (see also carrots; parsnips; etc.)

rosemary:
  black-eyed beans, rosemary, kale 170
  pumpkin, chickpeas, rosemary 114–16
  pumpkin, onions, rosemary 38
rose water:
  rice pudding, rose water, apricots 278
rutabaga:
  lentils, rutabaga, paprika 206–8
  parsnips, smoked garlic, feta 104
  rutabaga, mushroom, Gruyère,
    thyme 154–6
rye bread:
  apples, pears, rye 250

S
salads 132–3
  apples, blue cheese, walnuts 134
  beet, blood orange, watercress 136
  mushrooms, orange, breadcrumbs 138
  red cabbage, carrots, smoked almonds 140
salt:
  artichokes, winter roots, smoked
    salt 68–70
sauerkraut:
  beet, sauerkraut, dill 168
scones:
  chocolate, orange zest, candied peel 260
  parsley, parmesan, eggs 36
sesame seeds:
  tahini, sesame, butternut 188–90
shallots:
  chickpeas, radicchio, lima beans 90
  mushrooms, butternut, sour cream 180
  parsnips, shallots, goat cheese 102
  shallots, apples, parmesan 152
sherry:
  ice cream, chocolate, sherry 270
  sherry, blood oranges, cream 280
shortbread:
  hazelnuts, blood oranges, ricotta 266–8

soufflés:
  cheddar, tarragon, eggs 84–6
soups 164
  beet, sauerkraut, dill 168
  black-eyed peas, rosemary, kale 170
  Brussels tops, blue cheese 172
  carrots, rice, cilantro 198
  celeriac, horseradish, pumpernickel 174
  cheddar, cider, mustard 176
  fennel, cucumber, mint 178
  mushrooms, butternut, sour cream 180
  noodles, lentils, sour cream 182–4
  tahini, sesame, butternut 188–90
sour cream:
  beet, sauerkraut, dill 168
  mushrooms, butternut, sour cream 180
  noodles, lentils, sour cream 182–4
  red cabbage, carrots, smoked almonds 140
spinach:
  crumpets, cream cheese, spinach 50–2
  eggs, spinach, bread 54–6
  mushrooms, spinach, rice 214
  noodles, lentils, sour cream 182–4
  parsnips, cashews, spices 218
sprout tops:
  Brussels tops, blue cheese 172
  filo pastry, cheese, greens 146
squash (see butternut squash)
stews 164
  noodles, lentils, sour cream 182–4
stock:
  a brown vegetable stock 4
  winter stock 2–3
sugar, pistachio 256
sunflower seeds:
  artichokes, winter roots, smoked
    salt 68–70
  damsons, almond, sunflower seeds 262
sweet potatoes:
  lentils, sweet potato, tomatoes 94–6
  potatoes, sweet potatoes, cream 108

sweet potato, coconut milk,
  cashews 232-4
sweet potato, jalapeño, beans 124
sweet potato, puff pastry 158-60
sweet potatoes, tomatoes 126-8

T
tagliatelle, dill, mushrooms 236
tahini:
  mushrooms, chickpeas, tahini 98
  potatoes, tahini, thyme 110
  tahini, sesame, butternut 188-90
tamarind:
  eggplants, ginger, tamarind 14-16
tarragon:
  cheddar, tarragon, eggs 84-6
tarts:
  bananas, butter, puff pastry 252-4
  shallots, apples, parmesan 152
  (see also pastries; pies)
thyme:
  cheese, thyme, grapes 88
  orzo, smoked mozzarella, thyme 186
  polenta, thyme, Taleggio 226
  potatoes, tahini, thyme 110
  rutabaga, mushroom, Gruyère,
    thyme 154-6
toast 46-7
  beet, apple, goat cheese 48
  crumpets, cream cheese, spinach 50-2
  eggs, spinach, bread 54-6
  leeks, Caerphilly, mustard 58
  mushrooms, blue cheese, toasting
    muffins 60
  naan, mozzarella, tomatoes 62
tofu, radish, ponzu 42
tomatoes:
  black-eyed beans, rosemary, kale 170
  burrata, beans, tomatoes 20
  eggplant, tomato, coconut milk 196

leeks, tomato, Pecorino 150
lentils, sweet potato, tomatoes 94-6
lima beans, peppers, eggplants 74-6
mograbia, tomatoes, labneh 212
naan, mozzarella, tomatoes 62
potatoes, tomatoes, horseradish 112
sweet potatoes, tomatoes 126-8
tomato, chiles, udon 238

U
udon noodles:
  rainbow chard, egg, noodles 40
  tomato, chiles, udon 238

V
vegetables:
  a brown vegetable stock 4
  winter stock 2-3
  (see also carrots, tomatoes etc)

W
walnuts:
  apples, blue cheese, walnuts 134
watercress:
  beet, blood orange, watercress 136
wine:
  pears, red wine, Pecorino 276

Y
yogurt:
  apple yogurt 14-16
  fennel, cucumber, mint 178

ACKNOWLEDGMENTS

A heartfelt thank-you.

The messages by email and social media have been extraordinary. Heartwarming, generous, encouraging, each one has been gratefully received. The response to the first volume of *Greenfeast*, and the idea that "yes, this is how we want to eat now," has been life-affirming. That there are so many who wish to eat food that is predominantly vegetarian and plant-based, rather than meat-led or strictly vegetarian, has been welcome news. I want to thank everyone who has been in touch about the first volume of *Greenfeast* and to say that it is your enthusiasm that has led to this, the second volume, being finished on time.

That the books are here at all is due to the constant support and patience of everyone at 4th Estate, especially Louise Haines, my editor for as long as I have been writing. Thanks, too, to everyone at The Soho Agency and United Agents.

The recipes, as always, have been a collaboration with James Thompson, and it was once again a joy working with photographer Jonathan Lovekin, with whom I have worked every week for over thirty years.

The books are designed not just to look pretty on a shelf but to be used, day in day out, in the kitchen. Compact, tactile, easy to use. Books that look better with use. (I love the way a book settles in with use and opens flat at the most-cooked-from pages.) The fact that they are everything I hoped them to be is due to Tom Kemp,

Julian Humphries, David Pearson, Chris Gurney, Gary Simpson, Jack Smyth, and to everyone at GS Typesetting and Neographia.

While many recipes are new to this collection, several started their life in the pages of the *Observer* magazine, and I thank Allan Jenkins, Harriet Green, Martin Love, Gareth Grundy, and the entire team for their continuing support and encouragement.

Now, here's the thing. There is no point in anyone putting pen to paper, or more accurately, fingers to a keyboard, no reason for cooking and illustrating and printing and publishing, if there is no one to send those words and pictures out into the world. I want to shout a sincere thank-you to the booksellers of the world who continue to fill our lives with so much joy. The booksellers who look after our books, who embrace new volumes while keeping older, much-loved titles on their shelves, and especially those who recommend books to those of us who walk through their doors, hungry with anticipation. There is almost nowhere I would rather be than within the walls of a good bookshop.

Thank you, one and all.

Nigel Slater, London, September 2019

A NOTE ON THE BRUSHSTROKES

Many of us are placed on this planet in such a way that we experience all four seasons. For our cultures they constitute a deeply ingrained metaphor for growth and change, reinforced throughout our lives by seeing almost every plant (and certainly the ones in this book) attempting to reproduce itself annually, seasonally, in lockstep with the Earth's tilt and orbit. We even map the seasons onto our lives: as someone who has reached "autumn" I finally understand what older people have been telling me all my life and also the impossibility of any younger person understanding a word of what was said!

Spring and summer represent a forever forgetful beginning. The cold, barren enclosedness of winter is gleefully abandoned the moment the sun begins to rise higher and sooner in the sky. There is a looking-forward to the growth, energy, and abundance that are about to follow. The later seasons, however, tend to be soaked in a melancholy regret for all that exuberance and naivete; redeemed, certainly, by the warm, homely comfort of hibernation but also by the knowledge that longer, warmer days will come round again.

However, when it's one's life being measured by the seasons, there is no going round again. There is no undoing of the awful mistakes, no reliving of the youthful joy. There is a much deeper appreciation of what life is; a much bolder outlook on the importance of error, of hesitancy, of not having all the answers, of being more and more open to possibility.

The brushstrokes in this book are, again, not pictures of things. Each one is a record of a thought or feeling or simply a movement manifested through my use of a square-edged brush for a few concentrated seconds. They are informed by what came before, but they have a knowingness, a memory about them, that was not possible for those in the first book. I've let them be a little more idiosyncratic and sometimes not so sure of their path.

The square tip of the brush is like a large version of the end of the quill pen used by medieval scribes. The shapes it makes are mostly determined by the directions and angles I choose to push the brush around, rather than the pressure that informs the marks made with a pointed brush. Each brushstroke is ultimately derived from a letterform practiced over and over again to the point of abstraction, and together they define a kind of illegible but meaningful text.

It's a small relief to me to be able to record my existence in this very intimate and precise way for the very brief time the brush is in contact with the surface. These strokes are like deciduous leaves providing temporary evidence of the tree from which they fell.

Tom Kemp

A NOTE ON THE TYPE

The text is typeset in Portrait, designed by Berton Hasebe in 2013. Portrait is a modern-day interpretation of the early Renaissance typefaces, first made popular in Paris and cut by Maître Constantin. His influence can be seen in the work of the famed punch cutters of the next generation, Claude Garamond and Robert Granjon, whose work is so familiar to modern day readers.